THE PRACTICE OF TEACHING
A Positive Start

Bill Bennett and Kenneth Martin

Harper & Row, Publishers
London

Cambridge San Francisco
Hagerstown Mexico City
Philadelphia Sao Paulo
New York Sydney

British Library Cataloguing in Publication Data

Bennett, Bill
    The practice of teaching. – (Harper education
    series).
    1. Teaching
    2. Education – Great Britain – 1965 –
    I. Title   II. Martin, Kenneth
    371.1'02'0941   LB1025.2

    ISBN 0-06-318116-9
    ISBN 0-06-318117-7 Pbk

Typeset by Inforum, Ltd, Portsmouth
Printed and bound by A. Wheaton and Co Ltd, Exeter

To Joan, Jennifer and our children in appreciation of their tolerance of
many hours of 'teacher talk'.

ACKNOWLEDGEMENTS

Our thanks, for their advice and encouragement, are due to colleagues at Goldsmiths' College and to many teachers with whom we have worked; especially the late Bob Fordham. We are also particularly grateful to Aidan Warlow and Lynn Watkins, Deputy Warden and Advisory Teacher at ILEAs Ebury Bridge Centre for Language in Primary Education, and to Mrs. V. Webb, Senior Education Welfare Officer for Central Essex for their advice on aspects of Chapter Four. For the pegs upon which we hung Chapter Five, our thanks go to Sister Kathleen Walshe and Dr. G. Smith, Headteachers of Our Lady Immaculate School and Hylands School, Chelmsford. We are indebted to Mr. E. Riches, Headteacher of Beaufoy School, Vauxhall for permission to use figures 3.1 and 3.3, and to Mr. W. Uden, Headteacher of St. Thomas the Apostle School, Peckham for figure 3.2. Finally our thanks go to our typist, Lynda Bourne, both for her secretarial skills and for her patience.

PREFACE

In preparing for entry to the teaching profession the aspiring teacher usually follows a combination of 'theory' and 'professional' courses at a college, polytechnic, or university. Additionally he will carry out, under supervision, a certain amount of practical teaching in schools. It is well recognized, however, that in initial training it is impossible to prepare for every contingency that may arise when teaching 'full time' and the newly qualified teacher is often faced with situations and expected to assume responsibilities which he has not previously experienced.

Provisions for assisting the teacher at the start of his career vary from school to school and from local education authority to local education authority. Some teachers find themselves in schools where an experienced member of staff has particular responsibilities for giving guidance and assistance and/or where the local education authority provides specific induction courses. Others are less fortunate and may be unsure who they should turn to for help and advice.

Discussions with students and teachers in schools have pin-pointed a number of specific areas in which teachers embarking on and in the early years of their careers often feel the need for further information. While no one book can hope to bridge all gaps it is hoped that the topics covered in *The Practice of Teaching* will help to meet this need. Our aim is thus to offer practical suggestions while at the same time indicating the principles on which they are based.

CONTENTS

Seeking a first post – city, town or country school – denominational schools – state and independent schools – independent schools and the probationary year – the probationary year and teaching abroad – application forms and letters – the curriculum vitae – when offered an interview – advanced preparation – some points to look for in the school – the interview itself – questions, answering and asking – on being offered a post – contracts.

Before the term starts; advance preparation – the probationary year – initial contacts with pupils and colleagues – establishing good working relationships – marking and recording – work outside the classroom – responsibility and respect.

Different schools: common tasks, teaching and caring – induction – variation in complexity of organisation – the group tutor/class teacher, tasks and helpers – classroom communication and classroom management – some stage-related idiosyncracies – influential non-teaching colleagues.

CHAPTER ONE

THE FIRST TEACHING POST

During the final months of any course students are invariably surprised at the speed with which the time seems to have passed. Those preparing for teaching are no exception to this and are often heard to comment that 'it doesn't seem long since the course began and it's now time to apply for jobs'.

Before the process of requesting and completing application forms begins, however, there are certain issues which need to be given serious thought. Professional courses at college or university will have been geared largely to the teaching of a specific age-range of children and although it is possible for a primary-trained teacher to apply successfully for a post in a secondary school (and vice versa) such applications are generally not advisable for a first appointment. Certainly, however, some thought will have to be given as to where one should apply and why a particular area of the country has been selected. Some potential teachers – particularly, perhaps, those who are married and have family responsibilities – may have little choice as to where applications are made since it is usually necessary to take into consideration their husband's/wife's occupation and also the education of their own children. For others – probably the majority – the choice is greater and the major constraint is the availability of suitable teaching posts. It is as well to recognize that certain parts of the country have always had a greater attraction for teachers than others and, as a result, the local education authorities (LEAs) in such areas are usually able to fill the majority of their vacancies with teachers of some experience.

Do not therefore be too disappointed or take it as a personal slight if an application to one of the more well-favoured coastal sunny spots does not even result in an interview. By all means try – but be prepared! Generally speaking, however, there is a free choice and the choice made is likely to depend to some degree on personal preferences and the kind of environment in which you feel you would be able to settle down and devote your energies to the work in hand. The majority of newly qualified teachers are likely to take up a first appointment in or on the outskirts of a town. Some, however, will be attracted to working in inner-city schools and others may seek posts in a more rural environment. Applicants for posts in inner-city schools should, in particular, be aware of the demands which may be made in areas where difficulties increased by stresses resulting from inadequate housing or very low parental income are often manifested by children in their work and behaviour in the classroom. Also, many schools in our cities today serve areas in which the population covers a wide range of ethnic and cultural backgrounds. Whilst a variety of cultures represented in a classroom can and frequently does have a stimulating effect on the work of the school itself, the newly qualified teacher should be prepared for and sympathetic towards what may be required of him if he takes up a post in a school serving a multicultural community. If you feel reasonably confident – and particularly if your own education or teaching practices at college have given you some experience of city schools – then apply; you will find your work both stimulating and rewarding.

A contrasting environment may be found in rural schools where, particularly in the primary field, the number of children attending the school may be comparatively small resulting in correspondingly fewer teachers. Even today there are still small village schools with two teachers – and one of those is the head! Under such conditions it should not be difficult to 'get to know' the children and many teachers are attracted to such work. Remember, however, that lower birthrate in the country as a whole is at present having an effect on all schools and some of the smaller ones – in city, town, or village – have been or are doomed to be closed.

In all parts of the country there are also schools which represent particular religious denominations. Teaching posts are sometimes restricted to those who are practising members of the denomination concerned, whilst in other cases no such restriction is placed. In the case of the latter, however, the teacher who successfully applies for the post is expected, whatever his own beliefs, to respect the religious views held in the school and not to criticize or do anything to undermine practices which will form a part of the everyday life of the school community.

A final consideration for a smaller number of applicants for a first teaching post is whether to apply to the state or independent sector. Teaching practices will largely have been carried out in state schools and therefore, unless you have been educated yourself in an independent school, you will have little to help you in making such a decision. Usually classes are smaller (in such schools) but this is certainly not always the case. Some independent schools are boarding schools and to accept a teaching post will often involve undertaking additional duties outside of normal school hours. Applicants for posts in the independent sector sometimes assume that the pupils will have an almost angelic disposition towards education. Don't be misled – children are children underneath, whatever the uniform they may wear on the 'outside'! Two issues, however, need to be appreciated by the applicant to independent schools. Firstly, if you feel that you will spend your entire teaching career in independent schools then initial experience in such a school will be likely to be to your advantage. On the other hand, it is not always so easy to move from an independent to a state school – particularly if you have promotion in mind and where relevant previous experience will count for a great deal. Secondly, as discussed in Chapter Two, the first year of teaching after gaining initial teaching qualification is regarded as a 'probationary' one and, as far as England and Wales are concerned, probation can only be satisfied in a maintained school. Thus, the teacher who takes up his first appointment in an independent school and subsequently moves to the maintained sector will be required to successfully complete a probationary year in the state school. (This also has implications for those taking up a first appointment abroad as, with the exception of some British service schools overseas, a teacher will normally be required to complete a probationary year if and when he returns to this country.)

Having decided on the area or areas to which applications are to be made, the search for likely teaching posts begins in earnest.

The educational press carries advertisements both for specific teaching posts and for service within a particular LEA or, in the case of a large LEA, to a division within its area. Additionally, many authorities, and often even individual schools, write to colleges indicating likely opportunities for first-year students. Whatever the source of information of teaching post availability it is important that the method of application specified by the authority or school concerned is followed. Generally this will take one of three forms. A number of advertisements for teaching posts now indicate that the authority concerned is participating in the S.T.A.P. (Standard Teaching Application Proforma) scheme for applications. In such cases the application should be made using the 'S.T.A.P.' form which should be available in your college. The instructions for use are clearly given on the form itself, but note that you are expected to send a photocopy of the proforma to the authority or school to which application is being made and retain the master form. This will be needed if any further 'S.T.A.P.' applications are made.

A second method of applying for a post is to complete an application form specific to the authority concerned. Such forms will be obtained either at your college or by request from the LEAs to which you are considering making applications. As with S.T.A.P., the form itself should be completed with great care both in terms of the accuracy of answers and presentation of information. You are hoping to gain an interview and a prospective employer is unlikely to be impressed if it appears that little trouble has been taken with the application itself. Therefore, write clearly or type your application. The actual information required varies from one LEA to another but generally includes various personal details such as name, sex, age, address, and so on, together with some account of your own educational background and details of qualifications obtained. There is also frequently a space for the applicant to include further information which he feels might be helpful to a panel making an initial selection for interview. To leave this section blank might well be viewed as a rather negative approach on your part and it is thus worthwhile thinking carefully about what might be included here. Any particular interests or hobbies which you feel might well be employed in a school are worth a mention – in the primary field in particular an applicant able to play a musical instrument to a reasonable standard is often welcomed. Skill in one or more sports is also worth noting. Additionally, any experience with children and young people, such as assisting in a play group, Sunday school, or youth group should certainly be mentioned on the application form.

A final method of application, and one which is often required when a post in a specific school is advertised, is by letter supported by the applicant's 'curriculum vitae'. The letter itself should be fairly brief, stating that you wish to be considered for the particular vacancy and giving concise details of relevant interests as outlined above. The curriculum vitae is a summary of necessary personal details together with an outline of your career to date. Subheadings may well be used and for a first appointment the

submission can take the following form:
1 Surname followed by all Christian names and title.
2 Home address plus any holiday addresses and dates if applicable.
3 Age and date of birth.
4 Marital status. (Note, a married woman should also give her maiden name if she has taken her husband's name on marriage.)
5 Details of education and professional qualifications.
   a G.C.E. 'A' levels obtained.
   b Details of degree (where applicable).
State the name of the institution at which the degree was taken, title of degree, class, main and subsidiary subjects, and dates of the course.
   c Professional qualifications.
      i Give the name of the education department or college attended, dates of the course, and the title of the qualification obtained.
      ii Brief outline of specific courses followed during professional training (e.g., methods of teaching history, the teaching of reading, multicultural education, etc.).
6 Any relevant experience and/or interests.
7 Names and addresses of referees.
For a first teaching post it is usual to ask applicants to give two referees. Colleges and universities will normally supply a reference and the other should be someone who knows you well and is able (and willing) to comment on your character, ability and, possibly, potential. We say 'willing' as it is important that permission is obtained before naming someone as a referee. It does take time to write a reference carefully and it can be annoying – and possibly even embarrassing – to receive a request for a reference without previous knowledge that one's name has been used.

Before posting an application it is useful to make a photocopy which can be later referred to. Finally, it is well to note that not all LEAs or schools acknowledge receipt of applications and it is therefore wise to enclose a stamped addressed envelope if you wish to be certain that your application has been received.

After considering an application and references, a 'short list' is made of possible candidates and they are invited for interview. If the application has been made to a specific school the invitation is likely to come from the headteacher and the interview will be held at the school. If, on the other hand, you have applied to an LEA the initial interview may be at the offices of the education authority concerned. Those successful may then visit one or more schools. On receiving an offer of an interview it is important to reply immediately indicating that you will attend. A brief letter is all that is called for and can take the form:

Your address

Reference (as given on letter of Date
   invitation)

Dear Sir/Madam,
Thank you for your letter of 14th April 1980.
I will be pleased to attend for interview as requested on Thursday 24th April at 10.30 a.m.

Yours faithfully,

A Pedagogue (Miss)

The Headmaster

Address of School

If the letter of invitation was less formal, i.e., Dear Miss Pedagogue, etc., then it would be correct to reply: Dear Mr Smith . . . and end the letter, Yours sincerely.

In many instances candidates are invited to arrive in advance of interview times in order that they may look around the school and perhaps meet some of the staff. An invitation to have lunch at the school is also sometimes given. If such offers are made, they should, if possible, be accepted and your intention indicated in the above letter. Occasionally a candidate receives an invitation to attend for interview and is unable to accept for the day given. In such a situation it is equally important to reply immediately – and preferably by telephone – and, having explained the circumstances, ask about the possibility of an alternative date. This may well be arranged although it cannot, of course, be guaranteed.

Some advance preparation for an interview is generally desirable. First impressions do tend to have some significance and consideration should therefore be given to the clothes to be worn. Clearly there are no hard and fast rules but any style of dress which is likely to cause raised eyebrows all round is better avoided. The teachers' famous 'interview suit' (kept in moth balls for use at interviews and speech days) has much to be said for it on this occasion.

Although prediction of questions which might be asked by an interviewing panel has dangers and limitations there is at the same time some value in giving thought to areas on which questions might be asked. It is not at all unusual to be asked why you applied to that particular LEA or school. Questions on work done at college or interests outside of teaching are also popular. Primary school teachers would be wise to consider what their aims with a specific age-group might be and how the teaching of a specific skill, such as reading, might be approached. Secondary teachers should be prepared to discuss possible approaches to the teaching of their specialist subjects. Although the ethics of asking what contribution a candidate would be prepared to make to extracurricular activities have been questioned by a major teachers' union we must accept that at present this is an issue still raised by some interviewing panels. Remember too that at least the chairperson of the panel is likely to have your application forms and earlier we suggested that you should retain a copy of such forms. Now is the time to read through your application again – what information have you given which you might be asked to elaborate on at interview? Be prepared for this – an initial reaction on your part of 'did I really write that?' is unlikely to weigh in your favour.

On the day of the interview it is important to plan carefully in order to arrive in good time – to arrive in a flustered and semiexhausted state as a result of a 'last minute rush' is not going to enable you to show yourself at your best. If by any chance you are delayed then do telephone if possible and explain the reasons for the delay.

If you are being interviewed at a school first impressions are likely to be of the building itself and the environment in which it is situated. It is all too easy to be overinfluenced by either or both of them. What is important to appreciate is that to a very large degree it is the quality and professional commitment of future colleagues which makes a school in which learning and the personal development of the pupils can flourish. True, it is often – although by no means always – very pleasant to work in buildings which are modern and have been well planned, but buildings alone can never make a school.

Specific directions are usually given as to where to report in the school for interview. If this is not the case it is best to make your way to the general office and let the secretary know that you have arrived. At the same time keep both eyes and ears open as useful information may be gained. If lessons are in progress, what, if anything, can be heard? There are still teachers who appear to feel that everyone within a radius of a mile or so should be taking part in the lesson or that if a child needs reprimanding then only a 'sergeant-major-style dressing down' will be effective. Excessive noise emanating from the teachers may give some indication of the accepted style of teaching in the school, while excessive sounds from the pupils might suggest that the pendulum of control has swung too far in the opposite direction. By and large, however, it is not difficult to judge if a pleasant 'working atmosphere' seems to be the norm. If the school appears to be operating in total silence it may be worth wondering how and why this is achieved.

If the children are moving around the building either from lesson to lesson or going to the playground, then a further opportunity is presented to gauge acceptable standards of behaviour. When pupils are moving with due regard for themselves and others then this is a credit to the school and suggests that reasonable order is both expected and maintained. As with behaviour in lessons there are extremes. Some years ago a visitor to a large secondary school surprised her guide by commenting on the politeness of the pupils as they pushed along the corridor. 'Well,' she said, 'they do say sorry as they knock one over!' Such indications of lack of control outside the classroom may be indicative of a similar state of affairs during lessons. It is also useful to note if teachers are being approached by the pupils and/or vice versa. How do pupils and teachers approach and speak to each other? Is there an indication of mutual respect?

Finally, some notice should also be taken of the state of the building and the ways in which it seems to be used. Bare walls or walls adorned with graffiti are, like excessive litter on the floors, indications of standards accepted in the school. In primary schools in particular one would expect to see the work of the children on display both in classrooms and corridors. If there is little or none of this it is worth wondering why. Notice boards in secondary schools often provide a guide to the extent and range of house, sporting, and extracurricular activities which take place and are certainly worth scanning if one is given the opportunity before the interview takes place.

And so to the interview itself. There is, in fact, no set pattern for interviews and thus there are wide variations in practices adopted by different schools. Applicants in the primary sector may well have a single interview with a panel which can vary in size but will almost certainly include the headteacher, chairperson or a representative of the managers, and a representative of the LEA – frequently the adviser for primary education. Procedures in secondary schools are often more varied and it is not uncommon for candidates to have more than one interview, being seen first, perhaps, by the head of subject department, sometimes by a deputy head or another member of the senior management team, and finally by a panel of similar constitution to the one we have described for primary schools. An initial interview with the head of department is invaluable for both sides. He will be assessing how well he feels you are likely to fit into his particular team. From the candidate's point of view such an interview provides an opportunity to discover his likely duties if he were to be accepted, the range both in terms of age and ability of the pupils he would be expected to teach, and the facilities available for his particular subject.

Whatever the form which the interview takes, it is clearly necessary that the candidate takes every opportunity to present himself as well as he is able. It was with this in mind that we have offered suggestions for some advance preparation. Interview panels generally appreciate that candidates are likely to be somewhat nervous and make some allowance for this. At the same time it is expected that a prospective teacher has some (although not overexcessive) self-confidence and is able to answer questions clearly and thoughtfully. Muttered replies of 'yes' or 'no' to questions posed are unlikely to create the best impression and generally leave interviewers wondering how such a candidate is likely to fare in the classroom. Therefore speak clearly, look at the members of the panel, and give as full an answer as the question would seem to require. It is important also to be natural and not be seen as simply 'trying to impress'. This is not the place for lengthy quotes from the works of famous educators however well they may have been learned for final examinations in education! It should go without saying that all questions should be taken seriously as they will certainly be intended to be so. The candidate with B.A., B.Sc., and Dip. Ed. qualifications faced with a member of the governing body whose comment and question was 'that's all very well, but have you got your G.C.E.?' (yes we're told it really happened) would be unlikely to receive the vote of that governor if he answered with a burst of laughter! Occasionally a question may appear trivial or to have little point or relevance but the wise candidate will do his best to reply in such a way as to show that he has given it the same serious consideration as any other.

Towards the end of the interview it is often the practice to ask if there are any questions which the candidate himself would like to ask. Many appear surprisingly unprepared for this and as a result an opportunity for gaining information or clarification is lost. Although this is certainly not the time or place to enquire into the possibilities of rapid elevation to a deputy headship it is an opportunity which should not be missed for finding out more about the school's organization and practices. If information on the methods used for grouping children has not previously been given, now is the time to find out. It would, for example, generally be considered unwise for a firm advocate of streaming to take up an appointment in a primary school practising mixed-ability grouping. Many schools, particularly in the secondary sector, now occupy two sites. How does this operate? Would you be expected to teach on both sites and what provision is made for teachers doing this? One young science teacher impressed by the facilities for her subject in the building in which her interview was held accepted the post which was offered. It was only later, and much to her distress, that she learned that the greater part of her week would be spent at the 'other building' where laboratories and equipment were found to be far from satisfactory. A rather different issue worth raising if given the opportunity is that of rewards and punishments used in the school. Those who object to the use of corporal punishments can find themselves in an awkward and often upsetting position if they later find they have accepted a post in a school in which the cane is used freely. Clearly these are just examples of issues on which information might be sought and there are many others. The perceptive candidate will hopefully identify these and those who have given some thought in advance of the interview should have little difficulty in doing so.

After all candidates have been interviewed a decision has to be reached as to which one is to be offered the post. Sometimes this decision is made fairly quickly whereas on other occasions longer deliberation may be necessary. When two or more candidates appear to have similar merits the task of selection is by no means an easy one. Here it is worth emphasizing again the importance of a well thought-out and clearly presented application form or letter; a specific skill, hobby, or work with children outside of a school setting which has been mentioned in the application may be just sufficient to tip the scales in favour of one candidate rather than another.

It is often the case that an offer is made on the same day as the interviews and the successful candidate is expected to say there and then if he wishes to accept the appointment. (Those who have applied to an LEA rather than a specific school and whose application is successful will generally be allocated to a school as quickly as possible.) In the present situation of teacher employment many new entrants are prepared to accept without delay. Some, however, have other interviews arranged and would prefer to defer making a decision. All that can be advised here is to be honest with the school or LEA if you find yourself in this position. A few days' grace may be allowed but there is no guarantee that this will be given. We should stress, however, that a verbal acceptance on your part morally and professionally requires that you take up the post. Once an offer has been made and accepted, all other applications should be withdrawn as soon as possible.

A few words are due to those who are unsuccessful in that they repeatedly fail to be offered an interview or, having been interviewed, are not offered the post. It is understandable to feel demoralized and perhaps disillusioned – particularly after a number of applications have been made. The present state of teacher recruitment is such that some who have much to offer the profession are experiencing difficulties in obtaining employment immediately after qualifying. It is important, however, that those finding themselves in such a position recognize that they have not been rejected by the educational world at large and, however disheartening the process may be, continue to submit applications. In some cases it may be necessary for the applicant to cast his net wider and, unless personal circumstances prevent it, apply to areas of the country not previously considered. Additionally, it may well be valuable to look again at the content and presentation of information in applications and ensure that every detail which may be supportive is being given clearly and concisely to prospective employers.

Lest in attempting to be realistic we are accused of undue pessimism we must return to the procedure following a successful application – with the hope that this will be necessary for most of our readers. Once a verbal acceptance of an offer has been made, an 'official' letter confirming the appointment should shortly follow. Such a letter may include exact details of the terms of the appointment but the content does vary from LEA to LEA and in the private sector from school to school.

It would be true to say that many who have been teaching for some time would find it difficult to produce a contract of employment at short notice. In some cases a written contract may never have been issued. Today, however, those employed as 'full-time' teachers should receive from their employers a written statement giving details of the terms and conditions of employment. Such a statement should be provided within thirteen weeks of the teacher taking up his post.

Two copies of his contract should be given to the teacher; one he signs and returns to his employers and the other is retained for future reference. As we have noted, the contents of the statement itself and the order in which details are presented vary from LEA to LEA but should contain at least the following information.

1   Names of employer and employee. Title of the post to which the employee has been appointed.

2   Date of commencement of employment.

3   Whether any employment prior to entering the teaching profession counts as part of the employee's continuous period of employment with the appointing LEA. (This is important particularly for those who enter the profession after qualifying as 'mature students'.)

4   Annual salary and details of salary increments. (It is also usually specified that the salary will be paid monthly.)

5   Conditions relating to hours of work.

6   Holiday entitlements and pay.

7   Details of pensions and pension schemes.

8   Conditions relating to absence through illness.

9   The period of notice required if the employee wishes to terminate his employment.

10   Any disciplinary rules and procedures which may be applied to the employee.

It is important to appreciate that a contract is a legal document and should be read carefully. Reference may be also made in the contract to other documents which give further details of particular conditions. When this is so the documents concerned should be available at the school at which the teacher is employed.

Having thus secured his first post, the newly qualified teacher is usually filled with mixed feelings of elation and apprehension. What will be expected of him when he takes up his appointment? Will he be able to cope with the many and various demands which will be made upon him? Who might he turn to for help? We turn now to these important questions in the hope of providing guidance for the teacher in his 'early days in the school'.

CHAPTER TWO

EARLY DAYS IN THE SCHOOL

A new teacher has at least one thing in common with an old hand – a desire to be successful in his work. It can be dispiriting for the former to watch the latter at work; greater success than he has yet known is achieved, apparently with great ease. He may wonder if teachers really are born not made. But the 'old hand' is, by definition, one who has learned a skill so well, and practised it so thoroughly, that it now looks like second nature. He seems to use it successfully without conscious effort, but appearances are deceptive. If it is successful teaching, it will stem from perceptive planning and thorough organization. Watch critically the old hand at teaching and you will see that he has identified, and is carefully applying, certain principles. It will become evident that, before the session, he had:

1 formed a clear idea of what it was intended to help the pupils to achieve, and how.
2 surveyed the available resources, both material and human; selected from them appropriately, making good any deficiencies as far as possible; organized them mentally and physically.

So, once started, he is able to:

3 help the learners into 'attention',[1] prompting them to form the questions that make a learning situation, encouraging and aiding pursuit of the answers that constitute knowledge.

---

[1] 'Attention is best conceptualized as questions being asked by the brain . . .' Frank Smith, *Comprehension and Learning*, Holt, Rinehart & Winston, 1975, p.28.

Even while the work is going on, he is able to:
   4   evaluate all these aspects of it.[2]

This last is an essential prerequisite of further successful work on behalf of the pupils, and of his own professional development.

It is essential, then, for the newly appointed teacher to discover at the earliest opportunity certain items of information about the learning/teaching situation(s) for which he is to be responsible, to make it possible for him to manage them effectively during his first few weeks. If he uses the information to prepare well, his work will help his pupils to sustain or gain confidence in themselves as learners, and to begin to put trust in him. Such a start will have a beneficial effect on his own confidence, while he gains more information and greater understanding of the way his school is organized to meet its responsibilities to its pupils, and to help him to play his part with increasing success. If interviewed at an education office and appointed to the general staff of an LEA, the teacher may not know for some time at which school he is to work. If interviewed at a school and appointed immediately, he may be able to acquire some of the needed information straight away. In either case he is well advised to visit the school before the end of the term preceding that in which he is to start. Now that he is free of the tension associated with interviews it is almost certain that he will survey the school's environment more perceptively as he approaches, and assimilate better the advice and information he is given while he is there.

Perhaps the information to be sought first is about the timing of the school's day. The era of a common 9.00 a.m. to 4.00 p.m. day for all schools is gone. Quite recently, we found that the schools in one small area began their day at various times from 8.55 a.m. to 9.50 a.m. Some require staff to be in half an hour before the pupils, others only five minutes. The division of time during the day varies enormously; what is called 'a period' in one school would be referred to as 'a double' (lesson) in another. Assembly still begins each day in some schools; it crops up at sundry times in others. In an increasing number of schools, particularly at secondary level, a request for this information will lead to the teacher being given a copy of the school's staff handbook or guide. This should convey such important facts and many more. It is wise not to take too much on trust, however; it would be a remarkable handbook that told the new member of staff all that he needs to

---

[2] This four-faceted, apparently commonsense, approach to teaching has been developed as educational technology. For a clear and helpful introduction to its justification and practice, see Derek Rowntree, *Educational Technology in Curriculum Development*, Harper & Row, 1974.

know. Unless he is given a chance to consult it and discover just which of his many questions it will answer, he should carry on and ask them all. Even the best-prepared of handbooks will not tell him the age-range within each of the groups he is to teach. Neither will it give him a measure, formal or informal, of the range of ability. Both are needed as a basis for realistic planning. It would be unfortunate, for instance, to prepare a week's work which presupposed fairly developed literacy for any group which proved to contain a number of nonreaders. It could be disastrous at secondary level, where it is most likely to happen. It is also necessary to find out what kind(s) of classroom organization and activities the pupils are accustomed to. If they are used to working successfully in a fairly 'free' situation, it is not necessarily deplorable to plan a more teacher-directed régime, for a while. The teacher may need a little time, and a little help from others, the pupils among them perhaps, to be equally able to work in the more flexible way. The paradox of that kind of classroom organization is that, if it is successful, the freer the children are the more effort and skill the teacher has put into it. Sudden change in the other direction is definitely to be avoided. If the pupils are accustomed to having a teacher take all decisions about the content and organization of their lessons, they will need time and help to learn how to exercise any freedom to take them for themselves. This relates closely to a teacher's need to obtain clear information about:

what it is that he is required to help his pupils to learn first;

the physical environment in which the work will take place;

the resources that will be available for it.

For instance, his first thought about some particular learning that he must help the pupils with might be that the ideal medium for it is an audio-cassette recording in his possession. He would be pleased to hear that cassette players are available, but he would also have to take account of the information that his pupils are unaccustomed to their use as learning aids. Answers to the question 'What is to be taught?' may fall anywhere in the range of very permissive to totally restrictive. The teacher of infants who is the one most likely to work with the same class all the time, covering the whole curriculum, is also most likely to be given the greatest freedom to choose the content of that curriculum. The teacher in secondary or further education working, almost certainly, with several groups of students, possibly in a single curriculum area or subject, can expect least freedom to choose the content of his syllabus. The important thing is for the teacher to become fully and clearly aware of what he is to help his pupils to learn. Where there is freedom to choose, the inexperienced teacher should take the best available advice (see Chapter Three), and make the choice in good time to allow for thorough preparation.

Decisions about what is to be taught are, in ways that will have been explored in initial training, dependent upon the maturation and development of the learner, upon his interests and his capacity to be interested. Such decisions obviously precede questions about how the teaching is to be undertaken. Answers to these will depend upon the pupil's present status as a learner. They will depend upon what he 'knows' already, how good he is at recalling it and selecting from it relevantly. He has to choose from his 'theory of the world in his head'[3] just the ideas and information that will enable him to make sense of a new experience and to integrate it into his understanding. This is the learning that teaching tries to facilitate. But some ways of aiding it will not be available to the teacher because the physical context of the teaching precludes them. Clearly, learning through drama is not possible for a large group in a small room with nowhere, and possibly no time, to stack the furniture. Some learning experiences which should be possible in a given area may be devalued by the teacher's failure to take account of some characteristic of the area or its geography. One teacher learned this when, having prepared a lesson to take place in a familiar art room after morning break, he was asked immediately before the break to transfer it to another room. He did not look in the new room before the lesson. Consequently there came the moment when an otherwise well-prepared lesson began to lose all value for his young artists. With their interest aroused and keen to get on with the activity, they became frustrated by their inability to get at the necessary materials. The freedom of movement required to do so, in the way originally planned, was unattainable in the new teaching area. The new member of staff is well advised to find out where he will be working in the early days and to have a careful look at the possibilities of his teaching area(s). Particularly in the larger establishments, it is a good idea to note the route from the staff room to the place of his first assignment; it always pays to be on time for lessons, but especially

---

[3]   Smith (op. cit., p.11). The justification of this expression will explain also our parenthesis for 'knows'.

for the first one with any group.

As with teaching space, so with learning resources. By which we mean all materials and machinery, from pencil and paper to a language laboratory, by way of textbooks and television sets. It is noteworthy that one still sees more teachers harassed, more learning hampered, by the absence of a few sheets of paper, half-a-dozen pencils, or a pencil sharpener, than by the absence of a video-tape recorder. If the latter is needed it is seldom forgotten. Familiarity with the former, more simple, artifacts tends to breed a contempt which teachers really cannot afford. While he is exploring his teaching environment, the teacher must ascertain just what he must do to ensure that such humble necessities are always readily available to his pupils. Other software resources of crucial importance in most curriculum areas are books and pictures. It is important to discover the part played by books in his pupils' customary learning activities. If textbooks are used,[4] it is well to know how they are used. Copies should be borrowed to assist with the preparation of the first lessons, and the homework to follow it, if any is to be given. Whether it is and, if so, how, how much, and how often, should be found out. The availability of any good illustrative material relevant to his early teaching commitments should also be checked. So should other forms of software, e.g., transparencies, audio tapes, film strips. These would be useless without the associated hardware of course: in the case of our examples, an overhead projector, a tape recorder, and a strip projector. There is quite a range of such teaching aids now for a teacher to become familiar with. At this early stage, it is sufficient for him to find out whether any which he can already use and may want to will be available to him.[5] He will want to know where they are kept, and the system for borrowing and returning them. Similarly, if any part of his teaching programme is to incorporate any radio or television transmissions, he will need to know whether they must be taken 'live' or may be recorded; if the latter by what arrangement, if the former are they taken in a special teaching area. He will also need a copy of any teacher's or pupil's notes published to accompany the broadcast(s).

The teacher is very strongly urged, then, to find out what he will be required to do during the early days of his appointment, and when and

---

[4] For a succint introduction to the nature and value of flexibility in using reading ability, see D.E.S. – A language for life; Report of the Bullock Committee, 1975, 12.7–12.12 and pp.190–191.

[5] Some LEAs require a teacher to have a recognized certificate of proficiency in the use of items such as cine-projectors.

where he will do it, as well as some basic relevant information that will help him to get off to a good start. We have concerned ourselves with his curriculum tasks so far, but it is almost certain that he will have pastoral/ administrative responsibilities as well. It may be in this aspect of his work that he first meets any of his pupils. The ways in which schools organize and allocate such matters as registering their pupils and recording their attendance, as well as catering for other aspects of their welfare besides the academic, vary enormously in pattern and complexity. (See Chapter Three.) At this preliminary stage, the teacher needs to find out which register(s), if any, he will have to compile and/or maintain, and the where and when of their being obtained each day. If he can have one before him at the time, a short explanation will quickly uncover the not very deep mysteries of its marking. In the absence of verbal instruction, a glance at the flyleaf may be informative. The degree of separation between pastoral and academic responsibilities varies greatly from the scarcely noticeable in the infant school to the very deliberate in the secondary and further education sectors. The teacher should ascertain what nonacademic duties he must essentially carry out during the first week(s). If allocated what is often called a tutorial group, and timetabled to meet them regularly, he should establish what ways of gainfully using this time are prescribed or recommended, and what the group is, in fact, used to. To be valuable, these sessions require as much forward planning as any other (see Chapter Three.) There will also be supervisory/administrative duties of a more general nature, certainly in primary and secondary education, e.g., playground duty. One would hope that the new teacher is not required to carry out any of these during his first day at least, but it as well that he find out when his first duty will come, and where to look for guidance on how to carry it out before he has to do so.

When his initial training is finished a teacher can be strongly tempted to prepare less carefully for his teaching and classroom management. After all, he has shown that he can do the job; or has he? It is well to remember that judgements about the effectiveness of a student's final (and only?) teaching practice are, and can only be, judgements of potential; of how well he should be able to carry out the responsibilities of a full-time teaching appointment. He can never have borne quite this degree of responsibility in the student role; probably came nowhere near to doing so. His actual ability cannot be evaluated until he takes it on, until it becomes necessary for him to establish, and to maintain, effective working relationships with his pupils and all involved in their education; parents, colleagues, administrators, among them. How long any evaluation of a teacher's ability must be in terms of potential is open to question. Included in what one headteacher had to say to a young man in his first term of teaching was the following: 'Ask me after a year, and I will tell you if you will ever make a teacher; after five and I will tell you if you will ever make a good one; after ten, and I will tell you if you succeeded.' Without wishing to defend the accuracy of the later periods too strenuously, we would wish to echo the general sentiment. The wisdom of the initial proposition is recognized widely, and indeed officially in the requirement of the probationary year. By the time that he takes up his first appointment, the new teacher in primary or secondary education must have been awarded his teaching certificate, diploma, or degree with teaching qualification, a condition that will eventually apply in further education as well. He may be referred to as 'newly qualified', but this is misleading. He has to earn confirmation of his qualified status, and he only has his first teaching year in which to do so; in which to convince his employing education authority, on behalf of the Department of Education and Science, that he will make an effective teacher. The mechanics of the process of evaluation vary from one authority to another, but a common factor is the reliance of the inspector(s) charged with the task upon the reports of the headteacher. He, of course, relies to a degree that depends upon the size and complexity of his school, upon his senior staff for assistance in compiling his reports. The system adopted by many authorities would not be radically different from that used by one in the south of England. There, the headteacher is required to submit, by 31 October, a first statement of competence to the inspector with responsibility for probationers. The attempt is made to have every teacher visited by a member of the primary advisory team, or the appropriate subject adviser for older pupils, during this time, or before the second report is submitted at the end of February. Similarly, the inspector visits as many probationary teachers as he can, and certainly all that he must – those who appear likely to fail. The new teacher has external motivation to rely upon then, should the intrinsic weaken at any time during his early days in the school.

Almost certainly, as those early days come closer, the teacher's thoughts will rest increasingly on the instructional or pedagogic aspect of his work. All his anticipation, or fears, will be framed within a mental picture of himself shut in a 'classroom' with a group of learners, doing his teaching, or not, depending upon his 'discipline' or lack of it. We have stressed that this is indeed the most important facet of his work, but is not all of it. We have suggested that a minimum amount of information and guidance be sought during the preliminary visit to enable him to engage successfully with the system at first contact. It will now be necessary to turn this initial success into an efficient, positive contribution to the smooth running of the institution. It is not necessary to master all the complexities of the organization at once, but it is essential to make a beginning. Matters of immediate importance include such as the school rules, especially, in primary and secondary education, those relating to school uniform. That there are conflicting views about the need for school uniform is well known, and the teacher may not think it necessary. But, as a member of a team charged with maintaining the order conducive to the success of the school, he is not free to sanction breaches of the rules pertaining to this matter or to any other. Neither is it sufficient to look to their observance only in his own teaching areas or teaching time. They are intended to safeguard the welfare of the total institution; and any teacher who ignores a breach of them, as he goes about the school, is almost certainly ensuring that the next colleague to come that way will have a more serious one to contend with. A teacher's neglect of the rules is seen by the learners as contempt for those rules. Concomitant with the need to know the regular basis of the general discipline of the school is the need to know the acceptable ways to deal with any breaches of it, and the name and status of the next person in the chain of responsibility for its maintenance. Another aspect of the school's organization which will be of immediate importance is its timetabling. The teacher will already have acquired a personal timetable, but it is important that he find out where the general timetable is displayed and how to read it. This will be valuable in respect of seeing how his contribution to any learner-group's experience fits in with the rest. There is one aspect of this 'fit' that is crucial to good relations with colleagues. Every lesson of his that overruns its time and causes the next one to start late loses our teacher some measure of a colleague's goodwill. Of course, if the lesson runs into a playtime he is only losing his coffee – and the goodwill of his pupils. The master timetable is also important in connection with cover for absent colleagues. It is to be hoped that this particular duty will not be given to the new teacher in the earliest days. But, sooner or later, in a secondary or further education institution he will be asked to take group X for period N in place of Mr. Y. The master timetable will show him where the meeting must take place, and what kind of lesson the pupils will be expecting. Except in the direst emergency, he should have been given notice of the task in time to take advice from the appropriate head of department about what he might usefully work on with the group to minimize the effect of his colleague's absence.

By the time that this experience comes his way the occasions of his initial contacts with learners and with colleagues should be fading memories. In advance of those events he will, almost certainly, have been more apprehensive of close encounters of the former kind. He will want his pupils to be diligent and successful, the atmosphere of his classroom(s) to be orderly yet pleasant, even friendly. He may doubt that the latter reconciliation is even possible, while devoutly hoping that it will come to pass, somehow. The key to solving this problem lies in realizing two truths and understanding their relationship unambiguously. Despite the marked tendency toward a state of affairs in which 'No longer is the pupil's role clearly defined and circumscribed . . .',[6] with concomitant changes in the teacher's role, it remains the case that an orderly yet friendly atmosphere must be made, not prayed for. And, no matter how, or how much the teacher may share the task with the learners, the responsibility for it remains firmly with him. It is, as Marland makes very clear,[7] what distinguishes his relationship with the learner from those which the latter has with the other significant people in his life. It is a responsibility to the learner to make diligence and success in learning possible for him. It is to meet this responsibility that the teacher needs to establish good *working* relationships within and across the groups which he teaches.

The emphasis within our last sentence was placed with care. It may be noticed how many teachers seek to establish classroom relationships on the assumption that friendliness is all that is required for them to be described as good. It seems to us that while this is necessary it is not sufficient. Young people may find friends in many ways and friendship in many situations; the test of a period spent in school is to ask not was it pleasantly spent but was it fruitfully spent. As his pupils disappear from the room a teacher may seek to evaluate the lesson just ended by asking what, if any, benefit did they gain from it that they could not or would not have gained elsewhere. It is almost certain that the benefits offered by the lesson are more likely to be realized in a friendly atmosphere, but the value of a lesson which amounts to nothing more than a friendly chat is, at best, doubtful.

---

[6] Meriel Downey, *Interpersonal Judgements in Education*, Harper & Row, 1977, p.14.
[7] Michael Marland, *The Craft of the Classroom*, Heinemann Educational Books, 1975 (see chapter 7).

It is, of course, not unknown for teachers who are quite in agreement with our last statement to find themselves wishing that their lessons could achieve even the status of friendly chats, rather than incoherent disorganization. They come to class with clear, well-chosen objectives in their minds, but the pupils' minds seem to engage with these hardly, if at all. The pupils are often described as inattentive or distractable. We feel that their powers of attention are perhaps underrated and that their tractability is viewed from the wrong direction. They come to class in small clusters. These may properly be called groups for they are characterized by their members' attention being focussed upon, and by, an immediate shared interest. The individuals within each group are attentive to, and probably chattering about, some aspect of the lesson, playtime, dinner hour, or holiday just ended. They are less distractable than intractable. If they are to become a class group again, they must somehow be induced to forsake their diverse interests and to take up another, which by reason of being immediate and common to them all gives them a group purpose. The initial contact between teacher and pupils is crucial to this whenever a new learning/teaching session is to take place, but never, perhaps, more so than when it is to be their first meeting. That, above all others, is the time for the teacher to assume, in the absence of firm information to the contrary, that the members of the class have no ability to distract themselves or to refocus their joint attention to where he thinks it would do most good. This being so, it is for the teacher to divide and conquer. He must decompose the small groups by presenting each individual with a strong counter-attraction to the conversational joys of last night's television or last Saturday's local derby, and the sooner the better. For such a group the lesson begins outside the classroom door. In what is usually the more restricted area of a corridor it is that much easier to catch every eye and every ear. Very clear and detailed instructions can be given about what to do on the sheet of paper which is to be given to each one, and about where it is to be done. The handout would ideally serve the purpose of bringing the pupil's thoughts to bear upon what is to be the lesson topic. It might be any form of 'worksheet': questions to be answered, a picture to be drawn or finished in some way. It should draw upon what may reasonably be assumed as relevant knowledge already available to the pupils and the task should be one that each can accomplish. To ensure that they can physically carry it out the wise teacher will have with him a supply of pencils in anticipation of a chorus of cries of 'I aint got no pen, Sir'. And, as he funnels his charges into the room in single file, the teacher will ensure that his instruction to occupy the farthest empty desk is obeyed by each one. That prevents the 'playful' nudge being bestowed in passing, by the pupil(s), who, while being distracted from their recent concerns, have not tuned in to those of the teacher, and are still seeking alternative entertainment. These are the ones that the teacher will want to identify as quickly as possible, and the 'worksheet' will assist him in this. It is so much easier to spot when somebody is not paying attention to a piece of written work than to be sure that they are not listening, and so much easier to direct somebody back to work on a tangible paper-and-pencil task with leading questions and positive instructions.

We have attempted to describe a situation which we hope is not one in which a new teacher will find himself, but we have suggested one way of coping with it that we know to have a high success rate. More importantly we have tried to point to a principled basis for recognizing that a learning group has to be reconstructed every time it reconvenes, and that the member who has responsibility for it is also best able to facilitate the process. For us the major goal of education is autonomy for the learner. We would, therefore, expect the teacher to help his pupils to develop the ability to form themselves into a cooperative group until one day, being unavoidably delayed, he arrives five minutes late for a lesson with "the dreaded class thirteen" and finds that peace reigns. Most significantly, as he enters all take notice, accept his apology, and look as though they want the lesson to begin. When this comes about, it will be because the class has certain confident expectations of the teacher based on experience of working with him, and a confidence in themselves derived from that same experience. They will have become used to his lessons consisting of plainly justified, well-explained, well-ordered tasks to be carried out, which are just within their capabilities. Encouraged to become increasingly responsible for their own learning they will rely less upon the teacher's help, which is nevertheless always there when needed. In short, the factors we suggested as being fundamental to the successful start of a learning/teaching period, i.e., the immediate presence of relevant and possible tasks and the ready accessibility of necessary resources, remain crucial throughout the lesson; and in the success of one period lie the seeds of success in those that come after. However, this success will only flower if those lessons in turn are adequately prepared for.

The whole question of preparation is a vexed one. Many student teachers tear up their teaching practice notebook as soon as they safely may after their final teaching practice and never prepare for their teaching as scrupulously ever again. This is for most of us, ordinary mortals, a cardinal error. Preparing adequately for the relatively small amount of teaching done during initial training, and having to record it clearly in an appropriate way, is insufficient practice for the business to become a wholly reflexive affair.[8]

If we are ever to reach the point at which we can sufficiently record a truly adequate preparation for a lesson on a single sheet from a pocket notebook, we need to extend, well into our early teaching at least, the period during which we are subject to the discipline represented by the teaching practice notebook. That should never have been merely a window-dressing intended to impress outsiders. It should have been an instrument for increasing and recording the quality of lesson preparation; for ensuring that the marvellous learning experience that we thought up for our pupils last month/week/night is what they actually get today. If it was a vital professional tool during the comparatively leisurely periods of teaching practice it is certainly so during the demanding early days of full teaching responsibility. We offer the example of one teacher who set himself to keep, throughout the first year of his teaching in a primary school, a notebook exactly of the kind required of him during his final teaching practice. This meant that for each day he had to write up the preparation for each of two 'lessons' in full within the approved format. For all other pupil contact he had to write 'adequate' notes. We accept his claim that it was the experience of satisfying this self-imposed requirement that made it possible for him to reduce the time taken for successful preparation to a minimum very quickly; on transferring to secondary school, to be able to 'fill in' for absent colleagues at very short notice with something more satisfying than 'keep 'em quiet' tactics.

Although, in the time between accepting and taking up his first appointment, the teacher's thoughts may be most concerned with the prospect of meeting his pupils for the first time, he will wonder also about his first contact with his colleagues. The diplomatic ploy, which may have been wisely used during teaching practice, of trying to merge with the pattern on the staff room wallpaper will no longer be necessary or advisable. A certain degree of professional confidence will be looked for; but so, at the same time, will a proper restraint upon self-assertion. It is quite possible, but less probable, that quick and perhaps unfavourable judgements on aspects of the school, or upon its way of going about its business, will be accurate. It

---

[8] For suggestions of a variety of ways to structure and record lesson preparation, see e.g. Cohen and Mannion, *A Guide to Teaching Practice*, Methuen, 1977.

would be surprising if an equally quick airing of them was not resented. Intelligent questions are more likely to evoke early respect from, and acceptance by, colleagues than the most perceptive, unsolicited expressions of opinion, favourable or otherwise. By 'intelligent' we mean those questions which show that the newcomer is trying to understand the workings of his new school in the light of a relevant set of related ideas built up during initial training. These will reveal to his colleagues how well he used his previous opportunities for practice to ensure that his theoretical studies of education came into a proper relation with reality. We are fairly sure that, post-Bullock, no new teacher in a junior school being introduced to its reading programme will ask 'What is a phonic reading scheme?' We are quite certain that a more desirable effect will be produced when he says, 'I don't know that one; is it really completely phonic? May I borrow the teachers' manual?' While the new entrant to secondary teaching who says, 'Sets? What are they?', may sink without trace, the man who says, 'I have never encountered setting, but I did a practice in a school with full streaming; that should help shouldn't it?', ought to need no lifebelt. The non-professional aspects of first meetings with colleagues must also be considered. They may, even yet, be the more important. One must avoid the current equivalent of the archetypal staff room gaffe of planting oneself in the oldest inhabitant's 'own' armchair.

We have dealt, at what length we may, with the important business of first encounters and, in discussing such encounters with pupils, have already indicated how they might develop into good working relationships. We suggested that these would be based on the learners' developing confidence – in the teacher, and in themselves when working with him. Something very similar might be suggested for the development of good working staff relationships and we shall later extend the idea a little when considering the importance of nonteaching duties. We shall suggest that what is essential is an effective contribution to the maintenance of general school organization. First we return to working relationships with pupils.

One cannot overemphasize the importance of building a sound general classroom organization. In respect of this, primary teachers tend to have the advantage. Usually they have their own class in their own room. Additionally they teach the class for all or most 'subjects', often with a marked degree of latitude in deciding what shall be done and when. It is easier for them to establish the atmosphere of purposeful occupation that we have described as crucial, and to maintain it. An important factor in this is their total control of the quantity, siting, and accessibility of in-class resources. Concomitantly, it is easier for them to introduce items from the general resource bank into the classroom in such a way that they are available exactly when wanted without causing disruption, either before or afterwards. In short, they are best situated to provide an environment in which there is always something worth doing waiting to be done and the necessary tools available for doing it. They have the greater opportunities for enabling the pupils to become independent of them in, e.g., accessing necessary materials, or usefully occupying a spare moment when an ongoing task requires consultation with a teacher already engaged in the same with someone else. For the teacher who has a permanent teaching base shared with nobody else, to provide a departure point for a lesson in the form of some blackboard notes or in drawing, or pinning up, a picture is a simple business; it can be done while the pupils are busy in the preceding 'lesson'. Secondary teachers of some subjects are almost as well placed. In the nature of their subject it has to be taught in a specially prepared area, e.g., physical education, sciences, design and technology. The pupils meet the teacher on his own ground, and it is very much within his power to have the teaching area prepared in such a way that immediacy and continuity are marked features of the lessons which he offers. Provided that he is to use the same gym, laboratory, or workshop for both, he too can make preparation for a second lesson while the first continues. Additionally the scientist may well have the services of a lab technician in setting up apparatus, including any items that have to be drawn from the general resource bank rather than from the departmental collection. More difficult is the situation in which the pupils stay put and are visited in their home base by a succession of subject teachers. Much will depend upon what has gone before. To arrive at a classroom whose occupants have just spent a lengthy period of time being badly taught is to inherit someone else's problems. In such a situation the relevance of the first task presented to the learning intended is less important than its interest. Anything, within reason, goes. If it serves to restore the equilibrium of the potential learners, to increase the possibility of reconvening them as a learning group, it will have proved valuable. If it also wins a period of time during which soon-to-be-needed blackboard material or illustrations can be set out, so much the better. Teachers in further education are likely to have something going for them in this respect. Overhead projectors are more common in colleges of F.E. than elsewhere. If there is one in one's teaching room, preparing a transparency the night before is at least as good as getting to the blackboard before the lesson begins; better in that, by overlaying transparencies, one can continue to expand a visual display without the loss of eye contact unavoidable in blackboard use.

Unfortunately, the situations described so far are less common in secondary schools than that in which the learners spend little time in their 'own' room and it is occupied almost all the time by others. If the class teacher/ group tutor is alive to his task the room will not be uninviting. There may be drawings, posters, written work on the walls. Little, if anything else, is likely to be visible. Models left on exhibition tend to disintegrate even when handled with genuine interest by the constant stream of 'visitors'. There will certainly not be easy access to even simple writing materials. Such will be safely locked away, even carried away. Our new teacher, when in the role of group tutor, will himself have the same care about his own room and basic materials. In his role of teaching nomad he will be sure to carry a supply of things to write with and to write on. If in a school where, by edict, all written work must eventually be done in an exercise book, he will carry some, rather than just sheets of writing paper. A pupil whose very diligence has filled a book rightly resents having to do the first work in his new book twice, first on loose paper, to be copied into a tardily distributed book.

A proper respect for the products of the pupils' efforts is crucial to the development of sound working relationships with them. We have maintained that, and suggested how, they should be helped quickly to work, and kept involved and interested. What they do should be marked, and, more importantly, remarked upon, with a similar immediacy and continuity – and positively, i.e., with as much praise and encouragement as possible. The main reference point for assessment of an individual's present output is his most recent past work. Comparison of effort between individuals is reasonable. Comparison of outcomes is not ruled out, but it calls for the greatest awareness and sensitivity. One of the benefits accruing from preparing to keep pupils well occupied, and organizing to make them as independent as possible while being so, is the opportunity to engage more with individuals, to give them an immediate return upon and advice with their endeavours. Work then gathered up for scrutiny should be 'processed' and returned without delay. When returned it should have remarks upon it which clearly recognize and commend its strengths, and plainly identify and make helpful suggestions about its weaknesses. Criteria for assessment should always be clear and, where possible, negotiated with the pupils. What is possible in this matter will be determined more by the curriculum area involved and less by the age or alleged ability of the pupils. If we want eventual autonomy for our learners, the sooner we help them to practise making judgements the better. Because the teacher is called upon to make judgements about his pupils at regular intervals he should keep a careful and up-to-date record of all the interim assessments, formal or informal, that he has made of the effort put into, and the outcomes of, their work (see Chapter Three).

One other aspect of marking and recording must, however, be considered here: the travelling register. It is still the case that most schools use only the traditional register (Chapter Three). This can often wait upon the class getting down to work before being 'called' in a quietly unobtrusive way. Unfortunately, increasing truancy in some areas has led to the introduction of the travelling register. This follows the class/tutorial group and has to be marked each time it changes teachers; it can make a good start to lessons more difficult. It is, however, in very few schools laid down stringently that this document must be dealt with before all else. Obviously it cannot wait very long. If full advantage is taken of the time that it can wait, then it should be possible to mark it without destroying attention and concentration.

There will be various ways in which the new teacher may make a contribution to his pupils' experience of school outside the classroom. Some will be voluntary; about others he will have no choice. In both cases his participation can also aid the development of good working relationships with his colleagues. That he takes his share of certain supervisory duties is an obligation. Commonest among these is play/break-time duty. This may involve supervision of all or part of either the outside recreation area or the interior of the building(s). Not uncommon is the task of overseeing the movement of pupils from the premises onto buses after the schoolday. No longer obligatory, but equally important and to be carried out with equal care if accepted, is supervision of the dining area during the mid-day break. Whatever the duty it is vital that it be carried out completely and vigilantly. To arrive at the designated place punctually is essential; to ensure then that whatever is to take place does so in an orderly fashion and according to any rules laid down for it is equally so. At all times a teacher is expected to act *in loco parentis*. We have heard this translated as 'like an idiot parent'. Unfortunately, ignorance of Latin, like ignorance of the law, would not constitute an adequate defence against an action alleging failure to exercise proper care (see Chapter Six). Neither would it be easy to defend before parents or colleagues a failure to put forward one's best efforts to maintain standards of behaviour that they have worked to foster in the young people.

When it comes to nonobligatory duties, the task is in some ways more difficult, but more enjoyable and rewarding. No matter how dynamic and related to the realities and interests of the pupils' lives the school's curriculum may be, it will always leave room for their enthusiasm and awareness to be heightened and broadened by the activities of good clubs and societies. The value of a well-planned and organized, unstinting contribution to such activities cannot be overrated. A half-hearted, ill-organized, unreliable offering will do more harm than good. The difficulty lies in the adjustment of the participants to the differences in social atmosphere engendered by curricular and extracurricular activities. Pupils may tend to move too far from the formal towards the informal; some teachers may do the same. Problems then arise for pupils given a scope for action beyond their capacity to manage. Yet the situation should provide them with an opportunity to develop their social competence and this is lost if teachers cannot provide an atmosphere somewhat less constrained than even the most pleasant classroom tends to be.

The common characteristics of the relaxed and successful classroom and the thriving club or society are enthusiasm and discreet organization. Teachers should be offering pupils not a share of their knowledge but a chance to share the satisfaction, perhaps excitement, of knowing and of being curious to know more that has given them their enthusiasm for knowledge, general or particular. They should not expect their pupils to reflexively share their enthusiasm, nor to come to do so as a result of being told what the teacher knows and being asked to remember it for regurgitation at given moments. There is no satisfaction, much less excitement, in someone else's knowledge, only in one's own. The teacher's task is to cause the pupils to question something in their own knowledge, thus to become potential learners. He must make available to them ways of seeking, and sources of answers to, the questions they have formed or taken over as their own. It takes a thorough, imaginative organization of himself, his knowledge, and his resources to engender in the pupils the curiosity which can be the breeding ground of enthusiasm. The curiosity, even the enthusiasm, will already be in the pupil who joins a club or society. It should be treated there with the same respect as in the classroom. The resources, human and otherwise, available for its nourishment should be organized to be readily to hand and fully functioning. The latter can only pertain if the environment in which they are to be used is a stable one in which all concerned can work with confidence. The key to this is respect. We have referred several times to respect by the teacher, for the pupil, for his endeavour, for his products, but the respect has to be mutual. The teacher who gives it is entitled to expect it in return, and to expect that his pupils extend it to one another. The teacher who makes it plain that this is the way he sees matters, who can be seen to be playing his part, and who organizes the learning environment so that the pupils have a chance to play theirs will almost certainly have the pleasant successful classroom experience he hopes for. The teacher who makes no demands for cooperation and contribution from his pupils is neglecting his responsibility to their social education and asking for the disappointing experience he will surely have.

CHAPTER THREE

INTERNAL ORGANIZATION OF THE SCHOOL

We have seen already that, even when he is shut in 'his' classroom with 'his' pupils, the teacher cannot escape the fact that what is going on in there is only part of a much larger venture. That venture, the school, has become a complex organization because of the scope of its objectives, the variety of resources it calls upon, and the factors capable of affecting its progress. In schools having the smallest numbers of pupils, the complexity of the organization tends to be less obvious, but it is still there.

Everything has to be done to ensure that the pupils' experience of school is coherent, complete, and successful. Traditionally, British educators have taken a wide view of their task, seeing it in terms of the development of the whole child. Schools have developed curricula having not only depth and breadth of content but also variety and flexibility in practice. They tend to see this curriculum responsibility as one of two main divisions of their total responsibility to their charges. They discern also a 'pastoral' responsibility. This requires them to ensure a 'fit' between the pupil's various in-school experiences and between these and his out-of-school life, such that his individuality is respected and his all-round personal development is enhanced. This approach to the organization of school provision reflects the realization that, while a child's intellectual development may be considered apart from his physical, emotional, and moral development, it cannot proceed separately. The new teacher will have to be ready to see his pupils and his task in this way and to act accordingly. The comprehensive school whose organizational pattern is reproduced (Figure 3.1) is fairly typical of a large school in the way in which it shares responsibility within the staff and ensures cooperation with outside agencies. The probationer will have to become familiar with the organizational structure of his school to discover who contributes what to the well-being of the pupils, and who will help him to play his part. It may well be the particular responsibility of a senior member of staff to do just that.

The James Report in 1971 recommended that local authorities should designate members of school staff as 'professional tutors' to control induction programmes and to give help and advice to probationers. A government White Paper a year later proposed that probationary teachers should be released from one-fifth of normal duties in order to receive structured professional support and guidance in their first year of teaching. Pilot studies have examined the feasibility of such a procedure and it is hoped that induction programmes will be introduced nationally. In the meantime, provision by LEAs varies greatly in both respects. Some are still thinking about it. Others offer very positive assistance. One authority has appointed professional tutors and has an induction programme which is carried out partly in school and partly in teachers' centres under the supervision of advisers. The time allocated for it is one day each week at school and three days each term at the teachers' centre. Another authority stipulates that there should be one 'teacher tutor' for every three probationers, those for primary schools not to be members of the staff. Other areas recommend the designation of tutors but leave schools to make their own arrangements, which can be supplemented by assistance from the authorities' advisory staff or inspectorate. The most common practice in secondary schools is for a senior teacher or deputy head to assume the professional tutor role, but to share the responsibility particularly with heads of department and heads of house. In primary schools it is generally the headteacher who gives the necessary professional and pastoral assistance.

This is one indication of the way primary and secondary schools organize differently to do what is essentially much the same job. So the same organizing principles operate across the range of schools and, in general terms, all that might be said of one sector could apply to any other. But in their particulars the organization of secondary and primary levels have marked differences. Further, while colleges of F.E. most resemble the former, middle schools may look like either, or a mixture of both. We shall consider the various roles, including those that may be taken by the probationer, in each kind of school. We begin with those in the secondary school because, while its organization seems more complex it can be more easily illustrated, and because roles are more clearly defined there. Almost all that

Figure 3.1

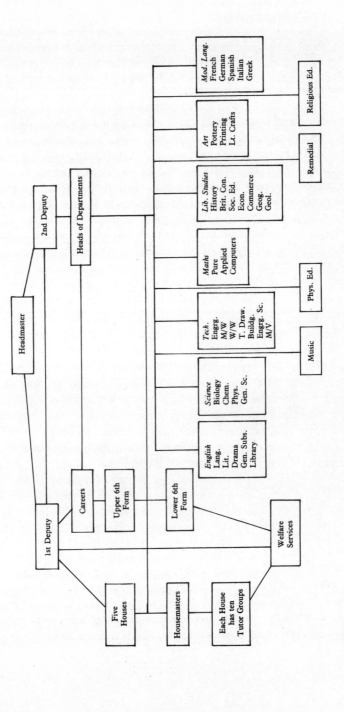

we say about them could be said without alteration, and the rest will provide a point of reference to aid clarity, when we move on to the duties of new teachers in primary and middle schools. We have already described Figure 3.1 as a fairly typical pattern of organization for a secondary school. It shows very clearly the paths of responsibility for pastoral and curriculum provision. The former runs, by way of the first deputy head, through the house system out to the welfare services. The latter runs through the second deputy and the heads of subject departments to the teachers of those subjects. The plan shows this more clearly than that of another comprehensive school (Figure 3.2), but the latter has greater scope and is more informative. In Figure 3.1 the focus is entirely on provision for pupils, and particularly that made by teaching staff. In Figure 3.2 it is made quite clear that somebody has special responsibility for probationers and who it is. It specifies some of the welfare services and shows more clearly their relationship with the school. It also points up the involvement of the nonteaching staff, although its format may not give a clear indication of their importance.

It is well to note that, although they appear to be at the bottom of the tree, their line of communication with the headteacher is apparently more direct than almost anyone else's. Lines of communication are not absolutely clear on either plan but, elsewhere in the staff handbook which contains Figure 3.1, the teacher is left in no doubt that 'regular and frequent communication between staff and head of house and head of department is essential'. A mimimum number of formal meetings in each half-term is prescribed as necessary for effective involvement and continuity and, lest a teacher might feel constrained to just those meetings, the nature and extent of other means of communication are set out as in Figure. 3.3.

This diagram, like the previous two figures, leaves no doubt that all authority and responsibility rests finally with the headteacher, even if today the former may be exercised democratically and the latter shared. It shows more clearly, however, the importance of the school secretary and her assistants to the efficient running of the school and, to the new teacher, as a source of information and advice about who does what, when, where, and how. As a final preliminary to looking at the probationer's role(s) in the school, it is interesting to note one more comparison between Figures 3.1 and 3.2. 'Careers' appear as a pastoral responsibility in the first but as a curriculum matter in the second. At first sight 'careers master' and 'senior master, public examinations' might have been accidentally transposed in

Figure 3.2

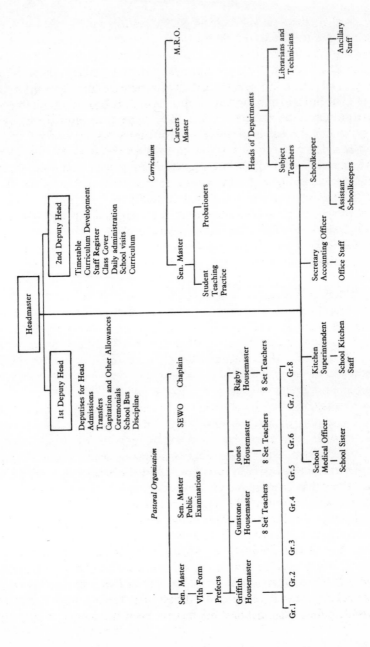

Figure 3.3

COMMUNICATION

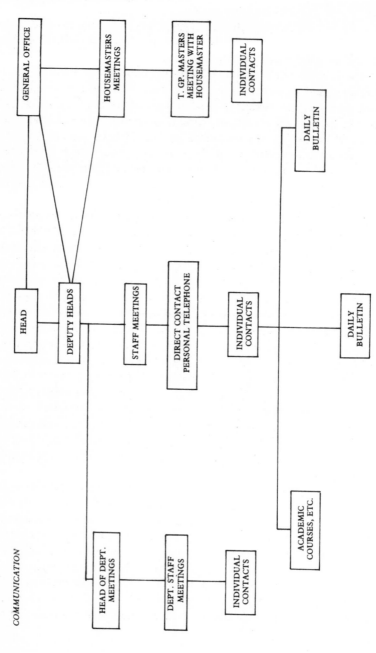

the latter, but further thought will suggest that this is not necessarily so. This may say something about the curriculum/pastoral distinction. The new teacher will discover that the distinction is more artificial than real. A probationer may well occupy two slots on Figure 3.1 or Figure 3.2. On either he would fit into the curriculum branch of the tree as a subject teacher, teaching his subject(s) to several groups of pupils. He may also appear in the pastoral branch, as a 'group' tutor in Figure 3.1, or as a 'set' teacher in Figure 3.2. In the former he would have general care of a mixed-ability group of pupils, in the latter of a group which is relatively homogeneous in a major ability. Often, as in this case, that ability is use of English. We will consider first the tasks he may have to carry out in this role and how he may relate to colleagues in doing so.

We have already characterized the pastoral aspects of a school's provision for each of its pupils as an attempt to ensure that his experiences of school be coordinated, not only with each other, but also with life outside school: the better to foster his personal development. The hub of this action is the group tutor, alias set/form/class teacher. However, before he can get on with the good work, he has basic tasks of registration. Every pupil's presence or absence, punctuality or lack of it, must be clearly and correctly recorded in the official register at least twice a day, at the beginning of the morning and afternoon sessions. Almost invariably, this task has to be carried out in the morning by the group tutor and, with almost equal probability, in the afternoon. It is sometimes the case that pupils go straight to their first lesson in the afternoon and the subject teacher registers them. It is also, in some cases, the custom for registration to be carried out as a preliminary, or aftermath, to a general assembly in the morning. In that case each group of pupils would have its own place in an assembly area and would there be registered. The more common practice is for them to gather in their own room.

As well as being an obviously useful document, the register is also a legal one. For both reasons entries should be made clearly and exactly according to instructions. The record of presence/absence, punctuality/lateness should be absolutely accurate. It could have to be produced in court as evidence of nonattendance. Such nonattendance may be for good reasons. It must always be accounted for in writing by the child's parent or doctor, no matter how short an absence it may be. We referred in Chapter Two to the travelling register which, in some schools, follows a group around from lesson to lesson. This is usually used in conjunction with absence report slips. One of these is filled in by the subject teacher for any absentee from his lesson whose absence seems unexplained. It will come to the group tutor. He may know that the absence was justified; in which case he will inform the teacher. Otherwise he will investigate and, if necessary, inform the head of house. Absence, long or short, unaccounted for or explained by dubious documents, should be investigated by an education welfare officer. The importance of the relationship between the school and this service is indicated by the position of the Senior Education Welfare Office (SEWO) in the deployment of pastoral responsibility in Figure 3.2. But the effectiveness of the service depends upon the officers being quickly informed of any reason for suspecting that a child's welfare might be at risk. Registers should, therefore, be marked only by a teacher, recording the presence only of pupils *seen* to be present, and be returned promptly to the office. Absence slips should be dealt with just as promptly. With equal rapidity the tutor should report to the head of house the absence of any pupil who has not been seen or heard of for more than a couple of days, whose explanation for absence is unconvincing, or whose absence causes the tutor any disquiet on his behalf. Truancy may arise from problems in school or out, and it will certainly give rise to them.

It is clear that the group tutor plays a crucial role in the school's caring approach to its pupils. If any external agency needs information about any one of them, the head of house will expect to get the most up-to-date and informed account from the tutor. The same would be true if the inquiry originated within the school. But a colleague worried about a pupil is more likely to go straight to the tutor for relevant information anyway. He must come to know the individuals within his group well. He will usually be helped in this by being their teacher for his own subject(s). The attempt is commonly made to give groups this continuity within their experience and to give tutors an extra dimension in their knowledge of their charges. Whether or not he teaches them himself, it will be for the tutor to find out, from their subject teachers and the organizers of clubs or societies to which they belong, all that he can about the members of his group in general and in particular. Such information is not best gathered by overhearing general staff room talk. That is often a safety valve for one's colleagues. If one believed all of it one's perception of some children or of some classes could be dangerously distorted. Spoken to individually and privately the same colleagues may well give a more objective and balanced view. Many schools operate a report system which alerts a pupil's teachers if he is having, or at least being, a problem with any subject(s). A pupil placed 'on report' will be given a form by his head of house. He will have to hand it to each of his teachers at the beginning of a lesson and they must write a comment on it at the end.

There is usually another opportunity, perhaps the most valuable, for a tutor to get to know the members of his group and to foster their development. It may be that the group convenes at the beginning of each session of the school day just long enough for registration to be carried out. On the other hand, one or other of these meetings, perhaps on every day of the week, may last for a whole teaching period. Certainly, most schools will include a number of such periods in the timetable for the group tutor to get on with the 'good work' to which we referred above. It cannot be emphasized strongly enough that the group tutorial must be used positively and energetically and with a particular objective, that is, to widen the scope of a pupil's personal world and to increase his desire and ability to be interested and involved in it. He must be encouraged to share interests in, thoughts and feelings about, people, places, and things with his classmates. Where appropriate and possible their deliberations should be accompanied by and/or give rise to action. The tutor-group session is not a time for doing tonight's homework, much less last night's. It is not only for pupils to be reminded about such things as school rules and school uniform, their justification and associated sanctions. These things have an important place in the group's activities; they are not all there is to it. What might there be to it? In alphabetical order:

Activities, e.g.:

Art (drawing, painting, sketching) – perhaps to illustrate

Books (diary, journal, log, narrative, scrap) – (devising, making, reading, writing) them for selves and others

Discussion (informal/formal) for planning, preparation, evaluation of projects, important issues

Drama (acting, design, play-production/writing) for its own sake, or e.g., school/house assembly

'Housekeeping' (making and keeping the group base a pleasant place to be)

Model-making (with conventional/scrap materials) for its own sake, to represent project outcomes

Content: people, places and things, here and there, now and then

People, e.g.:

Community/personal relations; give and take with friends, relations, strangers at home, school, club

Community service; long and short term, collecting and/or working for charities, emergency action, e.g., first aid

Personal service, i.e., to self; short and long term, health/hygiene, money management, hobbies and pastimes, evening classes and further education

Places, e.g.:

Our environment:

care about litter, pollution, vandalism

care for countryside, parks, public utilities/buildings

care of school, tutor room

school journeys:

'Where did he say we can go next term?'

'What's it like there, sir?'

local studies:

'My Dad reckons he must have cycled through our living room dozens of times, Miss. Mind you, it was a country lane then; the new town hadn't even been thought of.'

Things (abstract and concrete), e.g.:

Collections; Alice's/Tommy's cigarette cards/matchboxes brought into class for display, discussion, explanation, and comparisons

Current affairs; dissemination, discussion, evaluation, action upon, news or events at school, local, national, international level, of interest to, or in the interest of, the pupils.

Anybody looking in on tutor groups across the school, may find, e.g.,

an empty room, because the pupils are outside carrying out a traffic/market/amenities survey around the school, or

a 'mum' who is a nurse leading a session on first aid, or

an animated discussion of an item on the agenda of the next meeting of house/school council intended to brief the group's representative(s), or

a tutor informing the group about the functions of the youth employment officer and advising on the best way to use forthcoming interviews with him, or a quiz, devised and conducted by one or more of the pupils perhaps, or

a working party organizing the group's contribution to a forthcoming school charity drive, or planning ways of encouraging all their friends and relations to carry kidney-donor cards, or

a deathly hush as a group carries out a sponsored silence, or

a group of first-years, who are preparing a handbook about the school for children soon to come up from their old junior schools, being visited by a few fifth-years who are advising on design and will print it, or

a tutor making a point or two very forcibly about wear and care of school uniform, or

rehearsal of the singing, acting, reading that the group plan to do when they lead the next lower/upper school, year, house assembly, or

a thousand and one other activities.

We are convinced that the teacher's work in the group tutor role is at least as important as any he undertakes as a subject specialist. The group tutorial is not just a break between subject classes, and we reiterate our certainty (p.18) that 'these sessions require as much forward planning as any other'. Our examples of what the group might do, and how, give only some idea of the possible range. Even such a small sample gives us some important points for consideration. Social learning, like any other, is based in experience. Our examples, drawn from reality, show that pupils can be given opportunities to learn through experience of collaboration and sharing with neighbours, young and old, from within and without school. Current affairs at school level are vital. The pupils must feel that the school is really *theirs*. They can and must be kept clearly informed, and helped to be positively involved. With help they will be increasingly able to take an interest in, understand, and contribute to wider affairs. Ways of recording the learning outcomes of a variety of activities may themselves be varied. Tangible products such as wall newspapers, models, murals, collages, mobiles must be respected and carefully displayed. Material resources must be collected, organized, and stored in such a way that they can be secure but readily available. A pupil will not want, and should not be asked, to bring her collection of football souvenirs to school one morning unless she can be sure that it will be safely stored until she exhibits it in the afternoon. If necessary, the group tutor should be ready to take it into safe custody in the staff room. We saw that it might be necessary in a school where rooms are used/abused by a migrant population (Chapter Two). But such are short-term measures. For the long term it is better to go 'through channels' to get locks put on existing cupboards, if any, or to have cupboards fitted/placed wherever there is space in the tutor-group room. The system organized with the pupils for quick access to materials at the beginning of the period, and for even quicker putting away at the end, must include an arrangement for the cupboard keys to be easily available to the tutor's deputy if he is obliged to be absent.

The group tutor has, then, a responsibility, and opportunities, to get to know the individual members of his group well, to care about, and to foster their personal development. He is a key member of a team which includes a child's parents, his other teachers, their senior colleagues, and members of educational, welfare, and guidance services. He is in a position to observe a pupil developing an even firmer understanding, and control, of his/her world, being happy, energetic, and successful. He must be sure to reinforce this development by praise and encouragement; paying as much attention to verbal reports of success as he will to written notice of behavioural problems of less happy pupils 'on report'. His is doubly a vantage point. Not only does he have so much opportunity to observe his group but he receives a copy of all such reports. He will be the first to realize that what, to a number of isolated subject teachers, is a source of disruption in their lessons is, in fact, a child who is failing to learn in, or to cope with, school. Less certainly, he will be the first to realize that a particular child represents an even more serious behaviour problem. Like the disruptive, even violent, child this one is failing to cope with school, and possibly the wider environment. Instead of lashing out at his trouble he is withdrawing from it, and from reality. The latter is more certainly destined to occupy one of the one-in-three hospital beds taken by mentally ill patients than is the former. Recognition of such less obvious behavioural problems is unlikely to emerge from report slips. Teachers do not report 'good' pupils. The daily pressures can mask the significance of strangely docile behaviour. The tutor's observation of his pupils during contact time must be perceptive. If it gives rise to doubt of any kind about any child it must also give rise to relevant inquiry among colleagues. In similar fashion might the tutor come to realize that a particular child, while apparently quite happy at school, is nevertheless making no learning progress or giving evidence of serious underachievement. In connection with this eventuality, the tutor should be alert to the possibility of physical causes. The pupil who is 'failing' but well adjusted is unlikely to be a victim of child beating: one looks for evidence of that more in connection with the unhappy child. But he could be having 'fits', be partially hearing, or having problems with his vision. One would expect fits to be only too obvious, and the epileptic traumas that rightly merit that description are. We refer, however, to the milder form of epilepsy, less easily detected, that results in momentary lapses of attention or interruption of activity. It would not be surprising if the child with a partial hearing loss or sight defect got to secondary school before the condition was detected. Partial hearing loss may result in imperfect hearing of sounds on certain frequencies. This occurs most often on high frequencies, causing the hearer to lose or confuse consonants such as s, z, sh, f, th. Such hearing deficiency is difficult to spot because the child gets by in most situations, but it is crucial because the failure to discriminate between sounds, as in true/through, well/wall, is a handicap in learning situations. Clues to partial hearing loss which might still be present at secondary school include inattention, failure to respond to instructions or frequent misunderstanding of them, or turning the head to an unusual position when spoken to. The feature of such hearing loss that, perhaps, most makes it difficult to spot is that it may be occasional rather than constant, if caused by a nose/throat condition. Quite certainly, a teacher is never able, on classroom evidence alone, to be sure that the condition in present. Definite diagnosis requires an audiometric test. Equally definitely, any teacher suspecting that it is present should insist upon the child being given such a test.

He should react similarly if he observes any of the clues to sight problems, e.g., holding reading material at arm's length or squinting at the blackboard from eighteen inches, incessant blinking, inflamed or watering eyes. It is not safe to assume that any of these conditions will have been discovered at primary school; the child may not have been subject to it then. Once alerted to the probability that a pupil is, in any way, at risk the tutor must ensure that the suspicion, and the information which gives rise to it, travel as rapidly as possible to where they will lead to most good being done.

The group tutor should usually turn first to the head of house, or head of year. The former designation appears on both Figure 3.1 and Figure 3.2, but the head of year is not a feature of either of them. In many schools he forms a bridge between group tutors and head of house. In schools where the house system is fairly superficial, perhaps only a vehicle for intraschool sport competitions, he may replace the latter altogether. Then, members of a tutor group will not all be members of the same house, and the assemblies, for which their tutor has to ensure their punctual arrival, will be in year groups, if they are not of the whole school. In the same way that we have used 'group tutor' as a constant term synonymous with 'class/form teacher', we shall continue to use 'head of house' as being effectively synonymous with 'head of year', or 'year tutor'. We can be taken, then, as referring also to the responsibility of head of year to the pupils in that year, when we say that head of house has overall responsibility for the effective provision of pastoral care for the pupils in his house. He therefore has authority in the matter. Within the general framework laid down by the headteacher or a deputy, he will decide possibly when and where, more certainly how, assemblies, registration, and group-tutor meetings are to be conducted. In practice, most heads of house prefer to give guidance, rather than orders, to encourage initiative by the house teachers, rather than inhibit it.

We have said already that the head of house will expect the group tutor to be well informed about the members of his group. It follows that the tutor should keep complete and careful, even if terse, records of all that he learns about them. This will enable him to respond quickly and effectively to requests for information, or for comment on the probable reliability of reports from external sources. It will also ensure that, if the overall picture of a pupil's school life is a cause for concern, he will spot it. Scraps of verbal information may be easily forgotten. A series of such scraps over time may be perceived as separate, unrelated entities. Committing them to writing in a regular record maximizes the probability of their total significance being noticed. For similar reasons, while an approach to head of house for help or guidance, or to alert him to a pupil's possible/probable problem(s), might begin verbally over coffee in the staff room, unless it is so minor as to be dealt with there and then, it should be followed up in writing. There may be forms for the communication of information, requests, or requisitions. If not, a brief, precise memo will do as well. Communicating his disquiet about a pupil to head of house, even in writing, does not end the tutor's responsibility for ensuring that it arrives where it will give rise to effective action. If no reply to his communication is forthcoming fairly quickly, he should raise the matter again. It is for head of house to act on the information and to contact the appropriate service, directly or through the deputy head. One of them must make arrangements for any action thought necessary to be taken, and to inform the tutor. Such action may involve him in, for instance, a case conference of interested parties, or a consultation with the head of remedial education department.

In the absence of a clear instruction to the contrary, all requests for resources for the tutor-group activities should be made to head of house. Certainly he is the source of aid in cases of difficulty. It is he who, e.g., must agree that the cupboards mentioned earlier are necessary, and authorize their provision. Of course, if, at the same time as being asked for them, he is told that the caretaker awaits only his word before relocating some that are never used, the problem will doubtless be solved sooner. The teacher will soon discover that the Lord does indeed help those who help themselves, frequently through the agency of the two most influential people in the school, the caretaker and the secretary. More of that later. A last word for now about the working relationship with head of house, until, in Chapter Five, we consider writing reports to parents. In order to fully assist with the smooth running of the house, and be helped with his pastoral and administrative duties within it, the tutor must attend and contribute to its staff meetings. There he will hear of decisions taken at meetings of heads of house, and will have to agree with his colleagues ways of implementing them. But the communication must be two-way. It is for tutors to convey to the senior management team their evaluation of the current situation and their ideas for its maintenance or improvement.

We have been able to be reasonably specific about the duties of the group tutor and head of house/year. It is more difficult to be definite about the duties of any higher position, other than that of the headteacher. He must ensure, by judicious delegation of authority and appropriate supervision, that the school does its job. Those to whom he may delegate will be designated deputy headteacher, senior master, or senior mistress, the number of such posts depending upon the size of the school's pupil population. The only certainty is that there will be at least one deputy head. It is some time since we encountered a secondary school having no other post above head of house/year, but neither do we know many that have a senior management team quite as large as that in Figure 3.2. That figure does, however, with its lists of responsibilities delegated to each deputy head, show what duties the senior management team must share. The smaller the team, the more tasks the head will have to retain himself. These will be those that have least direct effect upon the day-to-day running of the school. The single deputy head will have responsibility for all else, although he will delegate some of the duties, probably those associated with pastoral care, to the senior teacher, if there is one. Most commonly it is not until there are two or more posts at the same level that a clear-cut division of responsibility, rather than of duties, can be seen. Then it is, most often, a division between curriculum and pastoral responsibility, the latter frequently being divided again into separate responsibilities for boys' and girls' welfare. It is for this reason that we said earlier, and we reaffirm now, that it is for the teacher to become familiar with the organizational structure of his school as soon as possible. Then, to take an example from the curriculum side of Figure 3.2, he will not bother a head of department or a senior master with the practical arrangements for an educational visit that he wishes a class to make: he will deal directly with the second deputy head.

Turning our attention to the curriculum duties of the new member of staff, we can return to a greater degree of certainty as we consider his responsibilities as a subject teacher, *vis-à-vis* those of a head of department. The latter has a definite responsibility for a particular curriculum area or subject. However democratically he may exercise it, his is a genuine authority in respect of the content of the syllabus, how it is taught, the requisitioning of appropriate resources, and the monitoring of academic progress. The class teacher must be prepared to turn to him as a source of advice and guidance and, also, to accept him as the originator of very definite direction. Neither the advice nor the orders should be accepted uncritically. If unable to resolve any doubts about them for himself, the teacher should put them to the departmental head. Advice may be disregarded if carefully considered and found truly unhelpful. Orders may never be flouted. They can be questioned further at departmental meetings, where policy should be shaped. Beyond that, a sincere belief that the policy is still inadequate in some respect could be communicated to the appropriate member of senior management, the head of department first being informed. The teacher may feel, for example, that the syllabus for first-years is too restrictive, overshadowed by the external examination still four years away. Or he may think that it never assumes a clear identity for the pupils, because it is taught only within integrated studies; that they begin their exam work under a handicap. Whatever the teacher's proposed change in policy, however good a case he can make out for it, he may not arbitrarily adopt any part of it.

While it is still true that, at secondary level, most teachers are required to teach only one subject, there is an accelerating movement toward their taking a wider curriculum responsibility, especially with the younger pupils. The division between pastoral and curriculum care has become somewhat suspect in their case. In the former situation, the teacher is responsible for several groups in one department, in the latter for fewer groups but to more than one head of department. As a group's subject teacher he must ensure that every member has maximum opportunity to carry out the programme of work laid down for it, each to the best of his ability. Whether the programme is a matter of agreement with, or decree from, the head of department, the teacher should be clear about what he is to teach weeks rather than days, months rather than weeks, before doing so. He should acquire formally from records, and/or informally from its previous teachers, some information about the group, i.e., how ready is each member to begin on, and succeed with, the programme. This amounts to finding out what relevant experiences they have had and what sense they seemed to have made of them. The information should be committed to writing, not trusted to memory. Since, when the time comes for the teacher and group to part company, someone will seek similar information from him, he should continue to keep a careful record of what the pupils attempt and how they succeed throughout their association. This usually lasts not less than a year. During that time, he will be asked at least once, possibly three times, to put in writing an evaluation of, and comment upon, each pupil's attainments and the effort that went into them. That the writing is done upon a report form to be conveyed to parents provides a strong extrinsic motivation to accurate recordkeeping, to which we will return in Chapter Five. There is another pressure towards it. As we saw, when we considered the duties of a group tutor, reliable information about a pupil may be needed by a colleague at any time. Most importantly, the teacher needs it himself, all the time. It may be that, in term 3, the group is to undertake some work that is logically dependent upon something done in term 1. It would be a good memory that recalled, with any great detail or certainty, just how each pupil had got on with the latter. If the teacher has two groups undertaking the same programme the task becomes harder. The difficulty is increased by the pressures on memory and recall during the early days of teaching, when everything about it is so new. He might not be able to recollect clearly which group did exactly what, or how well, never mind the attainments of individuals. This could occur between the first and third weeks, let alone the first and third terms.

Total loss of memory by pupils can occur in that short time as well. It certainly will, if under the pressure of his new responsibilities the teacher loses sight of the difference between teaching and informing or instructing. Telling is part of teaching, not all of it. It is something you do when somebody has realized that he is uncertain about something, decided what kind of information in general and which bits in particular he needs, and has asked you for them. Even then, if you think that the spoken word is not the best medium to convey the information, you do not tell. You may still ask him to listen but, perhaps to a piece of music, not your voice. You may ask him to look at, e.g., a demonstration of skill, or a picture. Perhaps you ask him to feel material of a particular texture, or to smell a particular chemical. Often, nonlinguistic communication is best. We all learn this during initial training but many of us go through a phase soon after, when the knowledge is not reflected in our teaching. This may suffer in various ways.

Spoken language is the form of communication most used in the class-room, Sadly, most of the talking may be done by the teacher. The temptation to talk pupils into insensibility is great, of course, especially for a new teacher anxious for good 'discipline'. While they are having to listen to you, or look as if they are, they cannot be getting up to mischief. Unfortunately, they may not be learning much either. Possibly, the only uncertainty they will identify will be how to keep you satisfied and tranquil. Their chief learning will consist of developing an ability to read the clues, given by your voice and gestures, to an aspect of your mind. They will become adept at spotting which answers to your many questions will keep you happy, and they will trot them out. They will have made sense of the situation. They will not necessarily have made much sense of what you have been talking about, much less have understood it as you would wish them to. They may have experienced you talking at them, when you thought you were talking to them, and should have been talking with them. It can easily be forgotten that purpose is very important to both ends of a communication. The receiver has to be as certain about what he is listening, or reading, for, as the sender does about why he is saying or writing something. Then he can know how to listen or read, and how much. He can also have some idea of which bits of his knowledge will help him to make sense of the communication, and can try to retrieve them from his mental filing cabinet. So, when a teacher begins to speak to a pupil and wants him to listen, he must tell him why. The more specific the teacher can be about the purpose, the better. Of course, if he wants the pupil to do something more demanding upon his mental capacity than receiving a piece of information, or carrying out a simple instruction, he could do more. He can arrange for him to talk about the lesson topic first, with some or all of his classmates. He will listen to the pupil sharing knowledge with them and sorting out his ideas. He may contribute the occasional question to help with this. The pupil realizes that he can already express a lot of commonsense about the topic. Then, if the teacher makes use of the understanding that has been revealed, when he starts to make his contribution to the talk, the pupil finds that he can also make sense of the matter, the way the teacher does. He finds that he can ask questions that even make the teacher think.

Teachers involve their pupils with written language quite a lot, too. The time spent on it is usually divided more evenly between receiving and transmitting, than that on spoken language. They are required to read *and* write. The trouble is that one can forget too easily that there is more to writing than wielding a pen, and more to reading than meets the eye. Subject teachers at secondary level are right to think that they should not have to teach their pupils the rudiments of reading. A pupil who is unable to read with reasonable fluency a text read with ease by his peers needs the attention of a reading specialist. Help should be sought for him (and for his teachers) from the school's remedial department and/or the advisory service (see Chapter Four). While the pupil is being helped to improve his basic reading ability, the subject teacher can provide him with texts he finds easier to read than those used more generally by the class. He can also foster the development of the basic ability as he teaches reading to the class. Yes, he *does* have to teach reading – the reading of his subject.

One way of looking at the business of learning to read is to consider it as involving skill-getting and skill-using. The subject teacher will be concerned mainly with skill-using, but his pupils being given help with this will also be engaged in skill-getting (better). Because he knows that having a purpose is essential to effective reading-for-learning, the teacher will help his pupils become better able to clarify their reasons for a particular read, to know exactly what they are looking for. He will teach them, for instance, that, given the task, 'Read Chapter 7, and answer the questions' (usually at the end of the chapter), they should read the questions first. Then they will know how to read the chapter. If a question is answered by a particular item of detail from the text, scanning is called for. If they need to gain a general impression of what the text is about, skimming is appropriate. If, sadly unusual for most textbooks, the question is a good learning question, calling for the exercise of judgement and formation of opinion, skimming followed by intensive reading is required. There is no justification for the common belief that all the responsibility for teaching this sort of thing rests with the English department. Consider only that different subjects represent different ways of thinking about the world and therefore of writing about it. The English teacher must help the pupils to become aware of variation in language dependent upon the situation of, and purpose for, its use. The subject teacher must help them to develop and benefit from this awareness within the context of his subject. He will teach them to be efficient in selecting texts, using them, and recording what they have learned from them.

One thing that he will teach them is that it is best to read the graphics first, the charts, diagrams, pictures. These are so informative, have so little redundancy, that, for some purposes, they almost remove any need to read the narrative. To be consistent then, he must give careful consideration to what kinds of writing he asks them to do, as well as to whether he should ask them to write at all. The learning they are doing may be best assisted, that which they have done best represented, by, e.g., drama, art, modelling, a talk, or a good think. If writing will serve, it may not be narrative that will serve best. It is the relationship we establish between objects in our world that is the most important part of our understanding of it. Those relationships can too easily be lost in a pages-long screed of notes. They are clearly represented by the arrows in a chart or diagram which can replace those notes in the space of a single page.

We have tried to show how, under the pressures of early days in teaching, it is easy to forget that:

1   there is more to the subject teacher's task than telling his pupils about his subject if he is really to help them to learn about it;

2   a crucial aspect of their learning and his teaching is the linguistic context in which they go on;

3   if the pupils are to become responsible for their own learning eventually, they must be taught *how* to use reading, writing, talking, and listening as ways of doing it.

The general principles that may be neglected as a result have been indicated. We wish to mention just two of the specific ways in which the teacher's work may be affected, for they occur so commonly.

The first concerns homework. Our concern here is not with whether the teacher should set it but with how he should do so. We take it as settled that, if the school ordains that homework should be given, it will be, in just the quantity that is stipulated. Unilateral declarations of independence in such matters will not do. (See page 20.) However, it is one thing to give homework that can be done in, e.g., the twenty minutes commonly prescribed for first-year pupils, it is another to ensure that they know *how* it can be done in that time and are able to do it that way (see the example 'Read Chapter 7 etc.' above). In class, the pupil can ask for the teacher's help, or the teacher can notice him going the wrong way about things. At home he is having to be an independent learner, as far as he is able. We suspect that the negative experience of homework which many children have contributes greatly, may even give rise to, a not uncommon disenchantment with education. It is brought about as much by their being ill-prepared for the homework, as by the homework being ill-prepared for them. It also follows, from what we have said about language, that, if a teacher wants to address an instruction or question to N pupils with any effect, he should ensure that N pairs of ears and N minds are tuned-in to it. If his 'Listen to me please' captures only N−1, there is absolutely no point in going on, until he ropes in the other one. This is especially true if the outcome of his instruction is to be a cooperative activity. If the instruction is to be carried out by pupils individually, and is a fairly short one, he may decide to proceed with it to the listeners and to deal with the dreamer separately. But, one way or another, he must avoid acting as if he is being heard, when, in fact, he is not even being listened to. Any suspicion that one of the faces grimacing in earnest concentration hides a mind wandering in reverie must be checked by appropriate questions, i.e., questions which test whether his meaning was understood, not just that his words were heard. The questions should be addressed to the suspected individuals, by name.

Our last sentence might be seen as stating what is obvious after initial teacher training. We believe that it represents another aspect of the 'knowledge' that can evaporate under pressure. For that reason we wish to amplify and add to it.

There is a lot to be said for learning the name of each pupil as rapidly as possible. Uttering that name can be like giving a tug on an invisible rope, by which you control his movements, mental and physical, within the class. It can pull him back into the swing of things if you see him wandering, in either sense. The tone in which it is uttered can tell him a great deal about how he stands with you at the time. Pupils should learn, very quickly, that their teacher has eyes like a hawk. If he makes a habit of calling praise across the room/gym/hall/lab/workshop to individuals or groups doing something well in the farthest corner, he will be teaching them just that. It is essential for him to remain aware of all that is happening in his teaching area at all times. He must move, observantly, among the pupils. When he comes to rest with a particular individual or group, he must place himself in such a position that he can see the remainder just by raising his head. It should be raised frequently, and, if there has to be somebody behind him, turned as well. It is characteristic of a new teacher to become immersed in some small part of the situation and oblivious to all else. Yet, almost certainly, he needs to keep more closely and constantly in touch with all aspects of the classroom situation than does the old hand who does it better. There is a higher probability of a pupil's attention flagging during his lessons. The extent to which a pupil will deviate from the lesson activities will depend mainly upon the measure of his interest in them. For this to be strong and durable he must be able to see some point in them that makes them worth doing, and be able to do them. 'Able to' must be taken to include both 'can' and 'may'.

He can see the point of the activities only if he already has some relevant knowledge. He may, only if he is given time, opportunity, and help to bring this knowledge and its relevance to shape at the forefront of his mind. He can do the activities, mental and physical, if they are ones he has done successfully before, a new combination of some of them, or a gradual extension of one of them. He may, if the necessary space, tools, time, and freedom from distraction are available to him. All these conditions must be met for the pupil to become, and to stay, involved in the learning activities. It has been a constant theme of this, and the preceding chapter, that, therefore, the teacher must plan and provide for them all to be met. The new teacher, by reason of being new to his task, and even newer to the school, is unlikely to do it perfectly at once. Hence, the higher probability of a pupil's attention to his task faltering, and the greater need for the teacher to be really aware of all that goes on around him. The wandering mind/fingers/feet of one pupil can be a source of just the distraction for the rest that the teacher wants to avoid. If he sees and stops it almost before it has begun, all should be well. If he can avoid it so much the better.

We have considered several aspects of this positive approach to classroom control. It is a positive approach because it rests on the notion that one should seek to establish a situation with which the pupils want to be involved and in which 'deviance' is their last resort, not their first. There is one important element of the situation, to which we referred in Chapter Two, about which a little more must be said: the element of time. We made the point that the timing of the beginning of a lesson is very important. Everything possible (and perhaps a few miracles) should be done to engage the pupils' attention with the lesson's purpose, before they have even a fractional opportunity to get involved with alternatives. We further suggested that, as well as immediacy, i.e., an immediate start on something immediately possible, continuity is also important, i.e., the constant availability of something to do which the pupils are able to do. What has to be avoided is immediacy and continuity becoming, or seeming to the pupils to become, rush and pressure. What they are told at the beginning of the lesson they are to accomplish by the end of it must be, and be seen to be, possible. The longer the overall time and the bigger the overall task, the more necessary it is for each to be broken into smaller parts. The pupils should see clearly how manageable subtasks can be matched to comprehensible divisions of the time. Perhaps the overall period is a whole afternoon. Then they might have it made clear just what needs to be done by half-way through, and at the end of, each of the three/four lessons, or two/three hours. The making clear is an example of a situation in which continuity requires a teacher to make haste slowly.

We have stressed the need to give instructions clearly, and to ensure that they are heard by all (genuinely heard, i.e., understood). The best way to instruct is, often, to get the pupils to instruct themselves, i.e., to work out from existing knowledge what to do. This is one of the many reasons for which teachers ask their very many questions. Answers to the questions should always be *waited* for. Give the pupils *time* to think. Try not to be frightened by the silence. It will not be easy. Another necessity of continuity is, paradoxically, change. The time-span of attention to a single task, or to a succession of tasks of the same kind, varies from child to child according to age, ability, and other personal factors. The younger and/or slower learning they are, the more often must they have a change in the kind of activity they undertake.

If the change from one activity to another has been thought out, and is carried out, carefully, it is a source of refreshment rather than distraction. There can be quite enough of the latter. A large secondary school may even have a tannoy system. A loudspeaker fixed to the wall of your classroom will suddenly emit calls to attention, followed by requests or orders to all or sundry. These things have been around long enough now for most schools to have them under control. The messages they broadcast tend to have some real importance. If this is not so in your school, our advice is to restrain the natural impulse to violence; use the departmental meeting to try to influence the matter. We wish that they would broadcast only life-or-death messages. Nothing short of that should be allowed to disturb the flow of events in a classroom. That being so the new teacher will attempt to dissuade colleagues from sending messages during lesson time. For the same reason he should not do it himself. Sooner or later one of them would become a matter of life or death – his own. The patience of the most charitable of colleagues must snap eventually. If the subject of the message is a genuine emergency, there is sure to be a prescribed procedure for dealing with it. The teacher should make himself familiar with such procedures before needing to use them. In case of fire, colleagues will, doubtless, be glad to be informed; but the procedure will hardly be to write them each a note. The person to be sent for if a pupil has an accident may not be a member of teaching staff. It is essential to know who it is and how to contact them rapidly. The key to an important aspect of life in the classroom is, again, forethought. Lessons well prepared are less likely to go adrift. Those that do will be rescued by teachers who know what strategies are available to them. Problems in preparation related to knowledge of pupils and syllabus matters can be sorted out with the head of department or a departmental colleague. The departmental technician may be a more valuable source of aid if the problem concerns departmental resources. If it is a matter of school resources, it can be taken up with the media resources officer (M.R.O. on Figure 3.2), or the equivalent in a smaller school. The M.R.O. is a fully trained member of nonteaching staff. His responsibilities usually include the setting up of a resource centre in the school, coordinating and maintaining the media resources, instructing teachers (and perhaps the pupils) in their use, and producing learning materials. There should be a need to send for him, or the technician, *during* a lesson only if a piece of machinery suddenly expires and must be substituted for. Do check before the lesson that any equipment set up for you is correct. Halfway through the lesson is too late to discover that the tape on the video-recorder is the wrong one. The best planning cannot be guaranteed to eliminate all problems. Pupils will still, sometimes, fail to accommodate to the class activity. Encouragement and persuasion failing to get them involved, sanctions may be needed. It is essential to know beforehand what sanctions are available to you; be sure the children will. If you are sure that the pupil's failure to enter into the lesson stems from lack of desire or effort on his part, rather than from poor planning or provision on yours, threaten to invoke the sanctions and, if necessary, do so. Do not threaten some punishment that the pupils know you cannot carry out. Stick strictly to the procedures laid down by the school. A pupil's parents have to be given notice of a detention. Be sure that any punishment is fair and appropriate, and seen to be so. The offender must be identified with certainty and only he should be punished. A whole class should be punished only if the whole class offended. Take care that the innocent are not punished incidentally. Prohibiting a pupil his games period may penalize fourteen other, quite saintly, members of a school team and their teacher as much as your deviant. The imposition of lines or copying out of a book may send blood pressures soaring in the English department. Corporal punishment, where it still flourishes, is surrounded by regulations. Almost certainly, one of these forbids a probationer to use it. All these matters will be covered in the school's procedures relating to discipline, which will also tell you what to do if a pupil's behaviour is totally disruptive of a lesson. Then you may have to send a message during lesson time. You should be sure, in advance of the need, to whom it should be sent.

This chapter began by identifying some common principles underlying the seemingly very different organization of the various schools in the system. Turning to the detail of such organization, as it effects the new teacher, we have looked first at the secondary school. Our reasons for doing so were that, compared to the primary school, its organization can be more clearly illustrated, and the teachers' roles more clearly defined. We promised that what we said about it would provide a point of reference when we came to consider the work of new teachers in the other schools. Points of reference may be used to establish similarities as well as differences. We have asserted that primary and secondary schools do, essentially, the same job. At classroom level, the tasks of the primary and secondary teacher are similar in more than just the essence. To a reader, whose interest and experience, even of a short teaching practice, is in primary school, this must have been obvious throughout this chapter. It may look as though we have less to say to her than to her secondary colleague.[1] This is not really so. We would want to say to her, about her role as class tutor, all that we have said

---

[1] We knew that to avoid possible accusations of male chauvinism, we should depart from our conventional use of the third person singular masculine at some point. During a consideration of the primary school, where women teachers are in the majority, seemed as good a time as any.

about the tasks and responsibilities of both the group tutor and the subject teacher, for it combines them. It is in the contexts of the tasks that the differences lie. These are not vast. A secondary probationer should also find relevance in our remarks, even before we return to definitely common ground at the end of the chapter.

Although the notion of pastoral care arose from developments in the primary school, it makes itself less obvious there. For its teachers, there is much less separation of pastoral and curriculum responsibilities. In addition there is much less differentiation within the curriculum itself. Not many of the subjects named on Figure 3.1 will be clearly identified in most primary schools, and those that are may not be taught separately. This is to say that, in two senses, the teaching is not usually subject-based. Rather than teaching one or two subjects to several groups, a teacher takes one class for all, or most, of its work, which tends to be project-based, i.e., 'integrated'. Not only are responsibilities less clearly differentiated at primary school, but authoritiy is less obviously delegated. Until fairly recently such delegation, in any terms, would have been quite invisible in most of them. Lately, there has been some realization that, while the headteacher is unquestionably omnipotent, she is less surely omniscient. However, it is still a minority of primary schools that have a clear plan of organization on paper at all, never mind in a staff handbook. The fact that there are fewer children in the school and they are smaller does not mean that the new teacher will need less help on fewer matters, for they are younger and there will be a greater number in her class. The lack of a clear pattern of organization may mean that she is less certain of where to find it. A reasonably obvious source of help in curriculum matters, similar to that given by the heads of department in secondary schools, may be available.

It has been increasingly recognized that, while there are good reasons to ask the primary teacher to be a Jill of all the curriculum trades, it is too much to expect her to be mistress of them all. It is becoming common practice to allocate responsibility for key areas, or features, of curriculum to a particular member of staff. Since the publication of the Bullock Report in 1975, the incidence of 'post-holders' for language across the curriculum, and for library, has risen significantly. Mathematics, physical education, and audio-visual aids are other concerns commonly thus singled out. Such 'post-holders' are, however, less clearly the bearers of delegated authority than the heads of department; theirs is seen more as an advisory role. Direction tends to remain with the headteacher who may choose to ignore their advice concerning developments in practices and resources in their curriculum area. They should be a source of valuable guidance for the new member of staff. Each should be able, for her own 'subject', to:

1   give clear, detailed information about what resources are available, and how their storage and access are organized;

2   give a precise introduction to:
   a   the school's written policy which coordinates the work of teachers
   b   the written programme of work for pupils;

3   advise the probationer on how to put the knowledge and experience gained in initial training to best use in her particular school;

4   help the teacher to develop her knowledge and to evaluate new practices and resources in the light of further experience.

The new teacher will be fortunate if the policies, programmes, and post-holders are such that these requirements can be fully met. She can be most optimistic about the first. Factors within the development of primary education led to a strong, intuitive distrust of policies and programmes, and antipathy towards committing to print anything that resembled them. There is a growing awareness, however, that neither necessarily robs the teachers of a genuine autonomy, nor the children of inquiry- and interest-based learning experiences, while both may enhance the learning and make the autonomy more real and more rewarding. For her needs in respect of 3 and 4 above, the teacher may need to seek further inside or outside the school for advice (see Chapter Four). Within the school, the experience and goodwill of her fellow class teachers may provide it. If not, she has the head or her deputy. It is not uncommon for a head to relinquish all the administrative chores she can to the deputy, in order to keep the curriculum reins very firmly in her own hands. Another, since she cannot forsake all administrative duties, will relinquish none, and will give a fair amount of curriculum responsibility to her deputy. Quite commonly, a deputy has no regular duty beyond those of a class teacher. She is kept reasonably informed about management matters, curricular and otherwise, but is rarely active in them, except when the head is not available. Whatever the arrangement, it should matter little which of the two a teacher turns to first.

T.P.O.T.—E

Each will have the ability, born of the experience of the largely undifferenti-
ated primary curriculum, to give a first answer to any question. If it requires
anything more, and the teacher has chosen inappropriately, redirecting her
to the other source of help will be a matter of only a moment.

We have seen that the primary teacher most of the time, and the secondary teacher when in the role of group tutor, will practise a form of
curriculum integration represented by the project approach to learning.
Each may be called upon to contribute to another form of it: team-teaching.
We waited to refer to it here because, sadly, it is in something of a decline at
secondary level. As the name implies, it requires two or more teachers to
collaborate in planning and providing a learning experience for a group of
pupils. Such projects can differ in any of several ways. We resist the
temptation to discuss the general and particular merits of their various
manifestations to consider only such constant characteristics as may be
discerned. It would be unusual for such a venture to be carried out over less
than half a term, or during less than two 'blocks' of time, e.g., two
half-days, in each week. In some primary schools the whole teaching
programme may be thus organized, i.e., it goes on all day every day.
Participating teachers are required to contribute not only their general
abilities but also the benefit of any relevant special ability, interest, or
knowledge they have. The pupil-teacher ratio is never greater, often smaller, than for conventional dispersal into single classes. But, of course, each
teacher has a responsibility to every pupil, and to each colleague. The
teacher group has to be a genuine team or the venture fails. They must meet
regularly and frequently, commencing to do so well before the work is to
begin, for planning purposes. They continue to do so throughout the
project to monitor and evaluate progress. Communication must be clear.
Decisions must be taken about, e.g., organization, content, resources, and
they must be adhered to. If these conditions are met by every team member,
the reward for a given amount of effort is frequently greater than for the
same amount in the conventional classroom organization.

There is another variation on the conventional teaching situation that is
possibly most used in primary school: the educational visit. Teacher and
pupils leave the school and set up educational shop elsewhere for a short
time. Our present concern is with what must be done to ensure that the
expedition is educational and that all pupils return safely. With the latter
objective in mind, the local education authority lays down strict regulations
governing the organization of such journeys. The teacher must discover,

well *before* the date of the expedition, what they are. They will stipulate a child-adult ratio, and how many of the adults must be qualified teachers. They will have something to say about permitted forms of transport. If the authority is one with a large fleet of school buses, private coaches may be proscribed. Costs will also be dealt with. One very good reason for taking the matter up with the appropriate senior member of staff, even before definitely writing the visit into a plan of work, is to find out how much, if anything, the school has in the appropriate fund. Complete and coherent preparation is essential, for pupils and adults. Teacher(s) must have made a preliminary reconnaissance of the location of the visit. This will include liaison with the appropriate staff in any public institution to be visited. Many have a permanent staff of qualified people running an education service. Teacher(s) and pupils together must work out clear purposes for the visit, and what must be done to achieve them. Any necessary sharing of tasks must be done beforehand. Tasks to be carried out, and questions to be answered, must be clearly written, for most convenience on separate sheets of paper and clipped to a board. Every adult should be supplied with a clear, concise, written programme and a list of the pupils for whom they are to be responsible. If the pupils are to bring refreshments, one rule worth enforcing is a ban on glass containers. After the expedition, there is always something to be done before it can be said to be complete as an *educational* visit. There were purposes; were they accomplished? Can we write/draw// model/act/sing/say anything that will express the satisfaction that the visit gave us? But strike a balance between squeezing all the educational value out of the journey and all the enjoyment of it out of the pupils.

There remain two sectors of education to whose new teachers we have scarcely addressed ourselves directly in this chapter: further education and middle schools. We have said that colleges of further education most resemble secondary schools. We believe that everything we have said about the role of a subject teacher in the latter has relevance for newcomers to teaching in the former, especially in their work with their younger students. The pastoral aspect can arise in a not dissimilar fashion on some course having a compulsory general studies element, but it is here that the most obvious differences lie. The tutor group is not common in F.E. More usually a teacher is personal tutor to a number of students. There will be no house or year organization, but possibly a student services department. The responsibility for student welfare will rest ultimately with somebody probably designated 'student counsellor', and it may arrive with him via heads of department. In the last analysis it is the same responsibility that we have described in this chapter.

Middle schools were supposed to provide an extension of primary education. A minority do not; they are secondary schools in everything but name. The remainder do to a greater or lesser degree. Some are primary schools in everything but name. The organization of others quite clearly reflects the idea that, while extending their primary education, they must also prepare their pupils for the experience of secondary school. Provision for their first one or two years in the school is organized in the same way as we have ascribed to the typical junior school. The remaining two or three years much more resemble time in a secondary school. The title 'class teacher' during the second phase will be synonymous with group tutor as we have used it, and distinct from subject teacher. A class teacher during the first phase will combine these two roles as we have described for the primary school.

We conclude this chapter by enlarging slightly on a brief comment made earlier about the members of the nonteaching staff, and by considering for the first time the role of another kind of VIP. Slightly tongue in cheek, we described the caretaker and the secretary as the two most influential people in the school. What sense could there be in that? The caretaker, or schoolkeeper, has responsibility for the care, cleanliness, and security of the school buildings and furniture. If a teacher wants to be on the school premises out of school hours, especially during a closure, he must arrange it with the caretaker. Arrive unexpectedly when one of his cleaners has just waxed your classroom floor and he will not let you in. Similarly, if you are in the habit of letting your pupils leave your room in a terrible mess, do not expect his goodwill. He will have to deal with the legitimate complaints of his cleaners who have precious little time in which to rid it even of 'clean' dirt. His goodwill is worth having. He can relieve a busy teacher of infuriating difficulties with his, and his pupils', material comfort in their classroom, or with the security of their belongings.

The secretary develops an encyclopaedic knowledge of all aspects of the school's smooth running. To her 'proper channels' and 'correct procedures' are an open book. Moreover, she not only knows where everybody should be and what they should be doing at any given moment, but usually knows also where they actually are and what they are doing. As a guide through the labyrinths of bureaucracy she has no equal. Make a friend of her and, provided that you do not impose on her goodwill, all administrative problems, and not a few others, are capable of solution.

One kind of problem which the secretary could not solve might be described as 'personal-professional'. Unusually, but possibly, a teacher might find himself, for example, quite unable to accept a duty prescribed by a senior member of staff, or to carry it out to that colleague's satisfaction. If they are unable to resolve the matter between them, both have the right, and one the duty, to take it to the appropriate more senior colleague. Each, of course, owes the other the courtesy of telling him that he intends to do so. The bigger the school, the more rungs of authority there are, and the more wise heads. Even so, however improbably, the problem could defy solution even when it reaches the headteacher. It could then find its way to the education office, or the the school governors/managers. These are the people who could give the lie to our statement that all authority rests with the headteacher. It might be thought more appropriate to consider their duties in relation to the school in our next chapter. We find that the majority tend to develop a caring attitude to the school which, in conjunction with their right to enter it whenever they like, makes them 'insiders'.

In some cases governors are even more clearly insiders; they are members of the teaching staff. If, as seems likely, the recommendations of the Taylor Committee[2] are made law, each school will have its own board of governors,[3] on which the LEA, the local community, parents, and the teaching staff will be equally represented.[4] The local authority will delegate to the governors as much as it can without making a nonsense of its ultimate responsibility for running its schools, and they to the headteacher, remembering that they have responsibility for the success of the school in all its activities. The Taylor Committee was convinced that there was no aspect of the work of a school for which the teaching staff should be accountable to no one, or only directly to the authority. It is already the case that, although the head and his staff carry out the day-to-day organization of the school and its curriculum, they do so subject to the general oversight by the governors/managers. These have a duty to monitor the way in which the school is developing, and a right to be consulted by the head on changes of school

[2] Department of Education and Science (1977), A New Partnership For Our Schools, H.M.S.O.
[3] At the moment primary schools have boards of managers, and two schools may share the same board.
[4] For voluntary aided and special agreement schools there will still be an overall majority of governors appointed by the foundation body.

policy in any matters of organization, curriculum, or discipline. They have three main ways of maintaining contact with the school and its work, in order to carry out their duties:

1   by meeting formally each term, when one of the main items on the agenda is the headteacher's report;

2   by attending school functions;

3   by visiting the school during the school day.

The headteacher has to be prepared to submit a comprehensive report. He must not only seek the governors' help in getting inadequate facilities repaired, renewed, or replaced, but also their approval of matters of pastoral care and curriculum development. They are sure to be concerned by a sudden upsurge in the number of entries per term in the punishment book, or of accidents recorded in the log. They are also entitled to know, e.g., why it is proposed to integrate the curriculum across the first two years in their 'sought after' secondary school, or to change the basic reading scheme in their 'prestigious' primary school. They have a duty to seek a justification which has clearly taken account of relevant factors as disparate as, e.g., the learning opportunities of 'bright' and 'slow' pupils, the cost of necessary materials, the qualifications/experience/commitment of affected staff, and examination results. A teacher should not fear that a group of nonprofessionals are going to tell him what to teach and how. On the contrary, unless his governors are unusually perceptive, they will ask too few, rather than too many, questions about curriculum matters, attributing to teachers an educational infallability of frightening proportions. He may have an opportunity to judge for himself when one visits his school. The meeting might take place anywhere in the school, even his own classroom, but it should never come as a surprise. Although governors may visit without notice, they rarely do. They prefer to offer the courtesy of making advance arrangements, even to the head who issues a 'come when you like' invitation to demonstrate the permanent perfection of his school. The visitor may choose not to enter any classrooms. Some governors are too conscious of their visit being a possible cause of disruption there. Others feel that, since it is not their task to 'inspect' the teacher or his work, there is no point in meeting him in his workshop. We feel that both are wrong. Given warning of the visit, the teacher can organize to minimize disruption. Moreover, his response to his visitor, since he is on his own and on his own ground, is likely to be more assured, and therefore more informative. The governor is, after all, trying to flesh out the headteacher's reports, to see, and feel, for himself how well things and people are getting on. While we think that a prearranged visit to the staff room at a 'break' time is very useful, giving an opportunity to discuss matters in some depth with the staff, we are convinced of the value of the one-to-one situation. It is a two-way communication, we are certain. The nonprofessional governor may be so only in as much as he is not in the teaching profession. Those that are not members of a profession are members of some other socially significant group, not least among them being those chosen from the parent group. They will be glad to be welcomed into a teacher's classroom, and to insights into his enthusiasm for, and experience of, teaching, especially as these relate to 'their' school. In return, they will be glad to have him pick their brains of some of the 'noneducational' wisdom they have accumulated, which may, in fact, give him fresh insights into, and increased enthusiasm for, his educational tasks. It is to be hoped that the quality of the advice and assistance that the teacher receives from the various sources within the school is such that it has that effect upon him. Whether it is or not, he should not neglect other sources which exist outside the school.

CHAPTER FOUR

HELP FROM OUTSIDE

Local education authorities employ people whose specific duties include assisting the teacher with his professional tasks or promoting his professional development. Some will help him with what we have called the curriculum duties within his commitment to the all-round development of his pupils. Others will inform and advise him on the social and emotional aspects of that development in individual cases. Help of the former will be given by such as inspectors, advisers, advisory teachers, teachers' centre wardens. Assistance of the latter kind will come from members of teams headed by the school medical officer, educational psychologist or psychiatrist, the senior educational welfare officer.

The Secretary of State for Education is responsible to central government for the effectiveness of the national system of education. Since he could scarcely do the job alone, he has the civil services of the employees of the Department of Education and Science. At its point of contact with the educational institutions the department has Her Majesty's Inspectors. H.M.I.s no longer work at classroom level quite as they once did, and the new teacher may see little or nothing of them. This is because much responsibility for the actual provision of the kind of education service that central government orders has long since devolved upon local government. County councillors, being as subject to human limitations as secretaries of state, also appoint an executive body charged with, among other things, the effective running of their schools. At its point of contact with the schools, this local education authority has its inspectors. If someone is interested in the effective functioning of a piece of machinery, he will obviously look it over every so often to see how it is going. The greater the interest, the more thorough the inspection. But, if one is responsible for *ensuring* the machine's efficiency, one will go further. If it is performing badly, every effort will be made to get it running smoothly again. Whether or not this is necessary, everything will be done to ensure that it will be found still working well on the next visit. The more complex the machine, the more demanding the task. Worthwhile inspection of a modern computer calls for a great deal of technical knowledge and the ability to use it perceptively. Moreover, even if it is functioning perfectly when the inspector arrives, he may feel a need to put in a lot of work on it. Advances in computer technology may be such that, without reprogramming and the incorporation of greater flexibility within its functions, it may soon be virtually valueless. More complicated, by far, than any computer is a school. A computer can be 'told' to change its ways and it will; it only seems to have a mind of its own, a school really does. Rather, and more complicatedly, it has several. Some of them may be even more tractable than the computer, changing their ways unquestioningly at the slightest suggestion. Some are totally intractable. Many are neither. The follow-up to inspection with them is much more demanding than the simple injection of a new brand of oil into a machine. They will not be reprogrammed, but they will 'reprogramme' themselves when they comprehend some good reason for doing so. They will not be ordered, they will be advised.

Inspectors of that complex human enterprise, the school, must also be, or be supported by, advisers. Factors within the origins and early growth of the British education system led to the inspectors' judicial function being emphasized and the advisory aspect of their role being underplayed and undervalued. There have been serious attempts to correct this tendency. Some authorities do not have any officers *called* inspectors, only advisers: but any advice given without a preliminary evaluation of the situation would be suspect. Every authority, then, has an inspectorate and an advisory service, although the degree of distinction between them varies from one authority to another. The number of inspectors, and/or advisers, and/or advisory teachers an authority has, and therefore the number of tiers within their hierarchical arrangement, will depend upon how much it wants, and can afford to pay, to ensure the effective running of its schools. Since it is usually with the bottom rung of the ladder that the new teacher makes initial contact, we need concern ourselves with only that level, how that contact might be made, where, and to what effect. If would be very unusual for an authority to have officers of all three designations. We will refer, from here on, only to inspectors and advisory teachers, for these most clearly represent the distinction between inspecting and advising; the titles could not be used synonymously. In the way that we have described, 'adviser' could be virtually synonymous with 'inspector', and there is a great similarity between the role and that of advisory teacher. The general aim of the advisory service is to foster curriculum development in schools, and professional development in teachers. Its members usually have a record of successful teaching based on a positive effort to expand their own practices and knowledge, and have shown an ability to share the benefits with others. Where they are actually designated advisory teacher, the service is usually organized to minimize any judicial function and to enable them to work with the teachers in the schools in a more sustained fashion than is usually associated with advisers. Quite possibly, an advisory teacher would visit a school on two or more days a week over a lengthy period, if the objective was a radical restructuring of an aspect of curriculum in both its content and its practices. In which case, the advisory teacher would almost certainly be of the specialist variety, with a particular responsibility for that area. A good example of this would be a primary school wanting to devise and implement a post-Bullock language policy with the aid of one of the advisory teachers appointed since 1975 for just that purpose. However, it is impossible to be dogmatic about the distinction between adviser and advisory teacher.

Members of the inspectorate and the advisory service may have a general or a special responsibility. The designation 'general' inspector/advisory teacher can be something of a misnomer, for it usually means general in respect of the curriculum, but specific as to age-range. That is to say that the inspector for primary (or middle, or secondary) schools would be concerned with the affairs of those schools in a general way, without regard to divisions within the curriculum, or distinctions between curriculum and pastoral matters. A special(ist) member of either team would be concerned with a particular area or subject of the curriculum, e.g., humanities, remedial education, science, art. The need for such specialists in secondary education has been seen for a long time, and they are still most commonly required to function at that level only. But a similar need has been discerned for areas of presecondary curriculum. Specialists have become more common at the earlier stages, without lessening the importance of the general inspector/advisory teacher to the teacher of younger children.

We have seen already that during his probationary year, some member(s) of the local inspectorate or advisory service may seek out the teacher and/or require him to join them at the teachers' centre for part of an induction programme. Induction or not, one of them, at least, will be interested in his progress, because they will be charged with deciding whether he completes the probation successfully. This initial contact will most commonly be with a general inspector; almost certainly so at presecondary stage. What if there is no formal induction programme, or it is provided entirely within the school? It is to be hoped that the contact will still be made, and made quite early. If it is not made by the appropriate inspector within, say, the first term, what should the teacher do about it? Perhaps, he should breathe a sigh of relief, offer a prayer of thanksgiving, and another of supplication that matters continue so for another two terms? We think not. That would be to overemphasize ridiculously the evaluative aspect of the inspector's visit, and to devalue, even trivialize his advisory role. The teacher has spent three or four years developing an interrelated set of knowledges and abilities in order to make a reasonable start in his profession. He is, surely, unwise to ignore any possible source of the kind of advice and assistance that will help to sustain and develop his work. If he gave only one year to his initial preparation, such an attitude is even less wise. It seems most sensible to invite the inspector, if he does not invite himself, or to seek him out. If the teacher wants to minimize the evaluative aspect of the visit, he could ask the advisory teacher instead. This will not eliminate evaluation, as we have already argued; advice given without a perceptive appraisal of the context in which it is given is surely worthless. The teacher should want some competent person to judge how well he is doing, especially if good advice will follow the judgement. It is natural enough not to want our efforts scrutinized by an 'outsider', especially if they are our first efforts, and an adverse opinion of them could materially affect us disadvantageously. However, in the case of almost all new teachers, any fears of poor appraisal which beset them are groundless. Very few indeed fail their probation. Of the rest, some have problems initially, and recovery from a bad start becomes increasingly difficult the longer one delays in seeking help. Even those who get off to a flying start can build on their strengths, and develop others, all the more quickly with the help of sound advice. Sources of this should exist within the school, as we have seen, but they are not always easily tapped. The value of the teacher's wanting to seek advice from his colleagues is dependent upon their being available to give it. Crucially, they are seldom able to spend time in his classroom. Sometimes this is possible, especially if there is an efficient professional tutor. Even then, it makes little sense to spurn, untried, another source of possibly valuable assistance. The teacher could ask the senior colleague, who is conscientiously trying to help him, to arrange for him to be visited by the appropriate member of the inspectorate/advisory staff. There might also be an opportunity for the teacher to make the first contact himself, at a teachers' centre – of which more later.

The comments and suggestions of the advisory visitor, however he may be designated, will differ from the advice to be found in the school, in at least one significant way. It is to be hoped that much of our earlier description of the members of the advisory service would fit the teachers' in-school 'adviser'. There would be the wide experience, with success based on retaining an evaluative approach to his own work. The senior teacher would draw upon this and his formal in-service professional development for his work with the new teacher. A good primary headteacher, or secondary head of department, will be able, like a general adviser, to give advice and assistance with matters of classroom management and teaching procedures common to all curriculum areas, including preparing materials and selecting resources. The departmental head will be able to give assistance specific to the particular demands of his subject. The primary school head will be able to discern any need for help from any of her post-holders and will arrange for it to be provided, as a general adviser might call upon the services of a specialist colleague. The vital difference, between the best of these in-school advisers and the 'outsiders', is that the former's width of experience is in the past. They may have taught in several schools but, in the nature of things, they can be teaching in only one now. Moreover, a fascinating paradox within teaching is that good teachers are promoted – to do less teaching. This is a fate shared by many who join the advisory service, but, nevertheless, they stay in very close touch with teaching on a broad front. It is their job to be involved with a number of schools at any one time. They are required, also, to keep themselves informed, in all manner of ways, of developments and regressions in teaching within their age-range or speciality, over a much wider area. The particular quality of their advice is that it draws upon a wider understanding of contemporary knowledge and practice than the most conscientious in-school teacher could reasonably be expected to maintain. Indeed, they should be one of his chief sources of reference. Disseminating knowledge of the best local contemporary practices and of those from farther afield is one of their chief functions. As well as conveying information between teachers they must also arrange for them to share experiences more directly. To this end they arrange a programme of in-service education. The conferences and courses, long or short, of which this is comprised may take place in any of the schools or colleges, but if there is a local teachers' centre, many will be sited there. By attending one of these, or just by going along to the centre to survey its facilities, the teacher may, as we suggested earlier, make the initial contact with an appropriate adviser, perhaps with the assistance of the warden.

Excepting any formal induction sessions, a probationer might feel it unwise to attend any courses during his first year. The shortest of these would probably consist of a two-hour session each week for about half a term, taking place after school. If the new teacher is being as conscientious about the planning and preparation of his work as we have suggested is necessary, and making a contribution to the extracurricular activities of his school, this may be too much for him. However, if there is a teachers' centre, he may well find that a visit to it without attendance at any course pays dividends. It may give rise to some practical help with the preparation of work. All will depend upon the quality of the warden and the resources he has managed to acquire during a period of economic stringency that seems to have gone on almost as long as teachers' centres have existed, and which has killed off not a few. Again, as with so many features of the British system, it is impossible to describe 'the' teachers' centre. Decentralization of responsibility leads to as much disparity in their quantity and quality from one authority to another as in any of the possible sources of aid for new teachers to which we have referred. What forms part of the services of the teachers' centre in one area goes on in a separate media resources centre in another, or maybe does not go on at all. We described, in Chapter Three, the work of the media resources officer in a school lucky enough to have one. They are probably in the minority. More frequently that kind of service would be offered to all the schools in a given area, by such an officer based on a teachers' centre. There will be found equipment for making teaching materials, e.g., transparencies for the overhead projector, slides of illustrations in books, audio recordings edited to particular requirements. It has to be the case that the equipment for using these materials has to be available in the school. It may be the case that the means of making them is also there, but what may be missing is the knowledge required to make the difference between good quality products and bad. The M.R.O. will have that. He may also have machinery to lend for use in school, and a library of, for example, films, video-tapes, slides, as well as superior facilities for multiple reproduction in various media. His may not be the only resource collection in the centre. One or two curriculum areas may be similarly served. These are, specifically, language (especially reading) and mathematics. Representative collections of resources in other curriculum areas are much rarer and, whatever areas are covered, the materials are not usually for borrowing. But knowing what can be available is to know what to ask the purse-holder at school to supply, or can be the inspiration for situation-specific, teacher-made materials. A crucial aspect of the functioning of the centre will be the opportunities it affords for teachers to share knowledge and experience, not only during formal courses but also informally. An essential factor in this will be the availability and personal qualities of the warden and his assistant(s), as well as their possessing the same qualities as a peripatetic adviser. These too should be seen at the centre, at least from time to time, and as we have suggested, the warden can be the agent of a meeting between a particular teacher and an adviser at the centre or in a school. By direct inquiry or by perceptive attention to the kinds of questions which a year's crop of probationers are asking he can also arrange a programme of in-service courses that they really feel are worthwhile. Things like that do not have to be left to chance, of course; the teacher can always tell the organizing warden or inspector which short course he would like to find in the programme for the first term of his second year.

It was always the case that a teacher could expect to have cause, sooner or later, to worry about some aspect of the learning or general behaviour of one of his pupils. Today, it will almost certainly be sooner rather than later. It is nothing new that many of the approximately three percent of children with I.Q.s below 70 are in ordinary schools. It might be better if they all were, but that is another story. Meanwhile, given the system that we have, these slowest learners are a source of worry for many teachers, especially the newer ones. It may be that some help and advice from a member of the advisory service with particular responsibility for 'special' or 'remedial' education will suffice to enable the teacher to provide adequately for his CHILDS.[1] At the same time certain aspects of the present condition of our society ensure that, regardless of the age or ability of his pupils, the teacher is much more likely to encounter some with serious social or emotional problems than were his predecessors. On current estimates, one in nine of the present generation will require psychiatric treatment at some time. A rising divorce rate and changed moral attitudes have presented many chil-

[1] A mnemonic for Child(ren) Having Individual Learning Difficulties. As a referrent for such children it is infinitely superior to 'Remedials'.

dren with serious problems. As one senior education welfare office put it, 'It cannot be true that every child comes from a broken home, it just seems like it.' The fact is that, from some four-fifths of a million in 1971, the number of single-parent families had risen to beyond a million in 1976, and is expected to reach one and a half million by the mid-eighties. At 101,000 the number of children in care is the greatest ever. They may be better off, materially if not psychologically, than the half million living in families with incomes below the official poverty level. The extent of overlap between this group and the half million who constitute the population of 'latch-key children', we do not know. At the same time, child abuse increases. Investigation within one authority indicated an increase of twenty percent in the sickening torture of young minds and bodies. Children who suffer the worst effects of such social conditions may present serious learning problems, behavioural problems or, more likely, a mixture of both. They could have reason to be grateful for the help of any of at least four specialist services besides their school: the school psychological service, the child guidance clinic, the school health service and, linking all these with home and school, the education welfare service. Because of the help that they might give him with his dealings with the children, the teacher, too, may be glad of the existence of these services.

For various reasons, including the increased incidence of social/emotional disturbance in children, all the institutions have had to review their contribution to the activity of child guidance and be ready to make changes. The development in schools of a deliberate, and sometimes complex, provision for pastoral care, of the kind we have described, is not unconnected with this. Further, the education welfare office (E.W.O.) attached to each school was once its school attendance officer. The change of title reflects the fact that he is concerned now not only with attendance at school, or rather with lack of it, but in a positive way with any personal/social problem of a pupil that might cause or be caused by it.

The general health of our school population has so improved that the number of full medical examinations which the children are obliged to undergo has been reduced to a minimum. The school doctor must still look for evidence of malnutrition, but is more likely to find it manifested in obesity than in emaciation. The school health service is able to pay more attention to preventive medicine and to aspects of health with particular educational importance. While it no longer needs to provide dental and optic care, it must ensure that parents are taking advantage of the N.H.S.

provision. In many areas one or more of the previously necessary physical examinations is replaced by audiometric screening to locate children with hearing problems.

Possibly most changed, and still changing, are the specific child guidance services, none more so, perhaps, than the educational psychology service. To put it that way may seem to imply that the interests of the psychiatrists, psychotherapists, clinical psychologists and others at the child guidance clinic are always easily distinguished from those of the educational psychologist and their respective duties within their particular area's child guidance service is always clearly defined and coordinated. That is not the case. It is still true that a psychiatrist is a graduate in medicine who has gone on to specialize in the study of emotional and motivational characteristics and personality, that psychiatry is a branch of medicine dealing with all forms of normal and abnormal behaviour. It is also still true that the basic qualification of an educational psychologist is a good honours degree in psychology, but that discipline has developed. When, if ever, it was only a branch of knowledge dealing with the structure and operations of intelligence, as some thought it, certain limitations on the work of the educational psychologist made sense. He could apply tests of general and specific ability and coach children who presented difficulties in any school subject, leaving any other treatment to the psychiatrist. Developments, including the mapping out of the field of clinical psychology, and the emergence of specialists in the area, indistinguishable, at first sight, from psychiatrists, made this division of labour difficult to sustain. The breakdown of this tension between the two kinds of specialists was hastened by the increased demands made upon the child guidance services, but is not yet entirely resolved; that same increased demand has given rise to a tension within the educational psychology service.

His particular interests in the pupil put the educational psychologist rather at a main point of intersection on the communication map of all interested parties. It is not surprising that his work, besides interacting with that of, for example, psychiatrists, psychiatric social workers, psychotherapists, also requires cooperation with teachers, paediatricians, educational administrators, for instance. It was possible for one local authority to list twenty-three different activities customarily carried out by the service for the area's psychologists to place in order of importance. Their top five, in order, were: location and assessment of children with special needs, seeing individual children, advisory work in schools, in-service training, work with parents and preschool children. It so happens that they were already favoured with the pupil/psychologist ratio of 5000:1 that has recently been strongly advocated, but is still a target, if not only a dream, in many areas. A psychologist having 10,000 in his school population might see matters differently. Assessment of a pupil for some form of special education is a time-consuming business; he has little time for any other casework, never mind training and advisory work. The tension within the service is between a desire to maintain a traditional child-centred casework approach to its tasks, and pressure to give more time and effort to advisory work in schools and elsewhere. All of which will help to explain the differences, from one area to another, in the kind and quality of the help to pupil and teacher that the service may provide.

We have already made the point in Chapter Three that, for all their skills, the multiplicity of specialized workers in the educational support services can do a pupil no good if they do not know that he needs them. We hope that it is now clear that bringing a child's need to their attention is not the end of the matter for a teacher. In the present social climate, while the services strive to adopt a preventive strategy, they will also want to make it possible for parents and teachers to cooperate in solving what are essentially long-term problems, for which there can be no instant solutions. Teachers must not only be vigilant in their daily contact with pupils to recognize problems of attainment or behaviour, but also prepared to cooperate in more clearly identifying and solving them.

The first step for a teacher may be, as we saw earlier, only a matter of carrying out his registration duties carefully: the E.W.O. will investigate any report of absences explained unsatisfactorily or not at all. Or it may be a matter of reporting to the appropriate senior colleague some disturbing aspect of a pupil's work or behaviour and, perhaps, a suspected cause. If this is, e.g., a deficienty of sight, speech, hearing, or diet, he may communicate directly with the parents, or request/suggest that the teacher do so (see Chapter Five). If it is child abuse, for example, the first contact with the support services may again be the E.W.O. That officer plays a very important part in linking home, school, and the other services, having direct contact with each in many cases. It may be that, in a case of low attainment, the first outside contact is with a member of the advisory staff, as was suggested above.

The next requirement is for the teacher to keep in mind that he has communicated his unease and to ensure that his warning has been heeded and is being acted upon. It is a simple matter to check whether young Johnnie has yet been examined by the optician, Mabel by the speech therapist, Charlie by the audiologist, but not always easy to discover what the results were. Johnnie and Charlie may not be wearing spectacles and a hearing aid respectively because they do not like them, not because, as they will tell the teacher, they do not need them. Or, maybe, Charlie's hearing has been found slightly suspect but an aid not thought necessary, provided that he always sits at the front of the class. He may not tell Sir because he is more interested in always sitting next to Harry. Moreover, especially in primary education, there may not be a front of the class, in the sense of an area always close to the teacher's voice. It would be necessary for the teacher to have the audiologist so informed, so that he might rethink his prescription. In a small way this illustrates the advantage of a team approach to identifying and solving children's problems. This is certainly to be hoped for when they are of a social/emotional nature, and especially when they are severe.

The teacher should not only be willing to take part in a case conference upon a troubled or troublesome pupil, but should hope for this to be the way in which the matter is to be approached. In this way a composite picture of the child and his situation can be built up. Moreover, the teacher and the parents can be helped to understand the problem, and can help to formulate a realistic back-up programme to the specialists' work – a back-up which they must provide. This approach is becoming more common, but we indicated above reasons why it is not yet general. There may still be areas where the feedback from referring a pupil to the psychologist is not much more than a set of test scores and a bald 'diagnosis'. The teacher should pursue the matter, insisting upon being clearly advised how he may best take account of the information that the tests yielded, and of the pupil's experience of any special teaching, therapy, or counselling in school or clinic which arises from it. If the outcome of the pupil's assessment by the psychologist is a recommendation for a special education placement the teacher will almost certainly get to know about it without any effort. In such a case Forms S.E.2 and S.E.1 have to be completed by the medical officer and the headteacher respectively. The teacher is sure to be asked to supply information for the latter. If this is not the outcome he will still have an information-dissemination task. He will have to ensure that the information that he has received or extracted from the support service reaches and is

acted upon by anybody else in the school whose work with the pupil should
be affected by it.

CHAPTER FIVE

CONTACT WITH PARENTS

Surprisingly few years ago, about a yard inside many school playgrounds one would find a noticeboard which read 'No parents beyond this point'. Today the notices have disappeared and, in most places, so have the ideas and attitudes that caused them to be erected, along with those that ensured that few parents would disobey the injunction. Teachers are more inclined to credit parents with the ability to think, as well as feel, about their offspring, and to articulate their observations and interpretations of their children's behaviour. It seems more widely recognized that teachers are able and willing to feel for their pupils, as well as to talk at them, and write cursory, uninformative reports about them to the parents. Both the parties most directly involved with our young people in their all-round development have a greater, more explicit, understanding of that phenomenon and of their part in it. Not the least important part of that understanding is the realization that the contribution that each may make to the child's development is more effective when coordinated with that of the other. A teacher's contacts with parents to this end are of great importance. The information exchange that may result can help to ensure that a pupil's experience of the allegedly related worlds of home and school is, at least, not too schizophrenic. Of course, the one who knows most about that experience is the pupil. It would seem sensible that he should have a part to play in the communication exercise of such importance to him, in either or both of its written or face-to-face elements. The aim is, or should be, after all to understand *his* feelings, to assess *his* abilities, and to identify *his* personal strengths and weaknesses, in order to help him to use or alleviate them, in order to ensure *his* future.

The most fortunate teacher will find himself in a school where teacher-parent contact goes beyond information exchange. Parents will be actively involved in promoting the welfare of the school, not only by raising funds, but also by contributing to the day-to-day life of the school in various ways. This is not yet the most common situation, but most teachers will find themselves in schools where information does travel in both directions between teachers and parents, both in writing and at meetings. It is still possible, however, to find a school with a less well-developed approach to its relations with parents. The latter will be invited to the school but only to those sorts of functions which permit little meaningful exchange between them and the teachers. The implication, intentional or not, is that they cannot usefully inform teachers, but must trust the school to manage their offspring's education, and to tell them occasionally how it is progressing. The prize-giving, or whatever, is to be evidence of the school's right to the parents' trust; the information to which they are entitled will be given in the annual/termly report.

The most noticeable characteristic of that document will be its parsimony; how little room it gives anybody to write anything. There will be a small space allocated to each subject or activity on the curriculum, small parts of which will bear an assessment of work done in class since the last report and/or the annual/termly examination. Whether the parent understands the assessments will depend upon his mastery of the literal codes often used to convey them, and of, for instance, the relative values of a grade at different points on the school's banding/streaming/setting system. There will be a minutely larger space for comment on these outcomes, the effort that went into them, and anything else of relevance. Another, equally inadequate space will be for someone with a more general responsibility, e.g., a class teacher or group tutor, to comment more widely. Such a format was adequate when all teachers and most parents thought that the latter's only possible contribution to their offspring's education was a motivational one. Such remarks as 'Has done well', or 'Could do better', were sufficient. The implications were respectively, 'You may pat him on the head' and 'This is your fault, you must take a slipper to him, or his Friday penny away from him, or both'. It was fairly safe to assume that, even if the parent did not actually take such action, he would think that he should. Even if he had the temerity to wonder whose fault it really was that little Charlie was not fulfilling his potential, the report form did not encourage him to say so. It only had a tear-off slip for his signature to indicate that he had received it. If he had anything to say about it he would have to 'make a fuss', by writing, or going to the school. The general parental feeling about that institution, based upon their own experience of it, would not allow him to do this unless enormously provoked. Then, since he had 'worked himself up' to it, what took place had more the nature of a confrontation that a consultation, certainly at the beginning.

Despite the decline in authoritarianism and the more humane character of schools in recent decades, this may still be the case when a parent visits a school whose procedures imply that it resents parental 'interference' in its pupils' education and considers its own contribution to be beyond reproach.

A teacher who sees education, even marginally, as something more than filling the empty heads of his pupils with knowledge, will find such a form of report rather frustrating. If he joins a school that also has a rather more lively view of the process, he should not suffer that vexation. He will probably find that an attempt has been made to construct procedures and a report format that allows him to:

1   convey traditional report information, and more besides, in a comprehensible way, and to comment upon it more fully and intelligibly;

2   share the wealth of parental knowledge about his pupils that can help him to establish a rational, fruitful relationship between their experiences of school and of the world outside it;

3   obtain a first-hand appreciation of school experience from his pupils.

We would like to illustrate this by reference to good practice in this aspect of their work by two particular schools, one primary and one secondary.

At our primary school, each child has a report book which follows him through the school. On the flyleaf of the book parents are told that:

1   their child will normally be the subject of a progress report once a year;

2   that after reading it they must sign it and return it to the school;

3   they may keep the book when their child leaves the school;

4   opportunities are provided during each year for parents to visit the school to discuss the child's progress;

5   the headteacher is always available to meet parents, but is always grateful for three days' notice if possible.

New teachers should note the importance of knowing just what procedures are laid down in their school for such occasional visits from parents. It is not uncommon that the parent must be received by a member of the senior management team, and may not go straight to the class/subject teacher. The new teacher should observe such rules carefully, not only to avoid affronting the head, but also in his own interest. His job is so demanding in the early days that he will be grateful to have energy- and time-consuming interviews that are not going to serve any useful purpose filtered out from those that are. If working in a school where no such rule operates, the new teacher may be well advised to have a more experienced colleague present at the first few of such meetings where possible. The presence of someone having greater familiarity with the various aspects of the school context can be helpful during the discussion, and such a one can be of help in assessing the interview in retrospect, especially the new teacher's part in it. Moreover, should the visitor prove to have arrived with a grievance, real or imaginary, and in an intransigent or even belligerent mood, the presence of a colleague could be helpful in several ways. If the new teacher remains very quiet and the experienced one insists upon hearing what the parent has to say, refusing only to listen to impolite remarks or unpleasant language, the visitor may well talk himself into a more amenable frame of mind, and make possible an explanation by the teacher and discussion between them. In the absence of such help, it is not sound strategy to attempt to argue one's point. One should ask the parent to come to the appropriate senior colleague, and set off, leaving him to follow or not. Such encounters are not an everyday occurrence. We referred in Chapter Three to the importance of the school secretary and the schoolkeeper. The latter is responsible for the security of the school. Our experience of visiting schools suggests that few people enter without being politely, but firmly, diverted to the secretary's office, if they are not seen to be heading there and are not known. No secretary worth her salt is going to mistake the mood of an irate parent and allow him to get to the classroom of an inexperienced teacher. We shall return to a consideration of the kinds of meeting suggested by 4 above, when we have given further attention to reports.

Pupils at our example comprehensive school also bring home a report book, or rather booklet, but it is a different one each time. It is made up of separate sheets for each subject/activity on the child's school programme, and one for his tutor's and housemaster's comments. These are all stapled together inside a semistiff cover. Like the primary book it bears information intended to make the grades used in reporting on the pupil understandable. In each case a literal scale from A to E is to be used. The parents of the primary pupil are told that A means excellent; B, very good; C, average; D, below average; and E, poor. In addition they are told the marks may be modified by a plus or minus sign. This, of course, leaves the vexed question of what 'average' means, and parents are told that most children will be graded C because 'most children are of normal ability'. The pupil is given a grade for each subject dealt with in the report, and one can infer that it is an assessment of attainment, but this is not made explicit. The secondary pupil, on the other hand, is given two grades in each subject, expressly for attainment and effort respectively. Except that 'below average' and 'poor' become 'weak' and 'very weak', the attainment grades are explained as for the primary report. However, the first report booklet is accompanied by a short letter which explains that, for all reports during the first two years at the secondary school, A indicates attainment in that subject in the top 12% of the whole year group, B, in the next 24%, and so on down to E, 'in the next', i.e., last 5%. Effort is assessed on a numerical scale from 1 to 5. Numbers 1 to 3 describe the pupil as 'exceptionally keen and industrious', or a 'Good, keen worker', or 'Of average industry'. Number 4 says that he 'Does not work as well as most', while Number 5 reports evidence of 'Serious lack of interest and effort'. The more specific meanings attributed to the grades might give the parent of the secondary pupil even more help with understanding the assessments. Such explanations should certainly help the teacher to use the grades consistently and it is incumbent upon him to ensure that he uses them to mean what the parents, and his colleagues, have been led to believe that they mean. In the primary book there is one last preliminary comment, intended to help the parent to interpret the report. Of children marked D or E, it says that they may be doing their best and that they will need encouragement rather than blame. The teacher does well to bear this in mind in all dealings with, or about, his pupils, including writing his comments on their reports.

On the reporting pages of the books in our example there is considerably more room for comment than was common in the traditional report. Before we give attention to how it might be used, however, we can consider further attempts to be helpfully informative. The first page of the secondary booklet has an entry clearly identifying the pupil's tutor group, the primary book the pupil's class. The secondary document has a space for the tutor's name to be clearly printed, so it would not matter if his signature beneath his comments on the same page was indecipherable as so many are. In the primary book, there is only the signature of the class teacher below the last section of the report, 'General Remarks'. This may be of much less importance than another difference. The secondary report deals with attendance by stating clearly the number of the pupil's absences out of the possible number of attendances; in the primary book it is only described, for example, as 'very good'. The secondary report comments on punctuality in this way, the primary one not at all. Given the significance of truancy it might be thought that attendance is more usefully described in the former.

When he comes to write his comments on the pupil the teacher must make them inclusive of all significant facts within his particular concern. They should include any relevant information which is not reported separately, such as homework. The secondary report which we are using as a reference point has a space at the top of each subject sheet for the question, 'Is homework satisfactory?', to be answered yes/no/variable. In the extra space that this affords him, the teacher might want to indicate just how the homework is unsatisfactory, for example, or whether it varies in quality or punctuality of submission. In some ways there is less need to elaborate on the grade for attainment unless it has fairly clearly identifiable divisions. Our primary report example has, in addition to the general remarks section, four subject sections. Three of these are under a general heading 'Basic Subjects', and one of them is English. This is subheaded 'Oral', 'Written', and 'Reading'. There is a space in the grade column for each of these to be assessed separately, but the remarks' space is not divided. Such a format helps the teacher. Without it he would have to remember for himself the importance of the three aspects of language development, and use some of his space to indicate how much each one contributed to an overall grade for English. As it is, he can concentrate on relating the attainment to the effort, with reference to the pupil's manner of approaching, or attitude to, the subject, and to the context in which the learning and teaching take place. The various aspects of these are likely to differ in importance from one subject to another but significant ones might include neatness, patience, forethought, adaptability, socialibility, ability, and willingness to work cooperatively or to see a purpose in all, or part, of what goes on. Whether making specific comment as a subject teacher, or wider comment as a class teacher or group tutor, one must remember that the report is intended to give parents a picture of their child's all-round development over a stated period. They want to know how he has progressed academically and socially in curriculum and extracurricular areas of school experience. The child's inabilities and disabilities will be obvious enough in the grades; do not hammer them home in the body of the report. Refer to the progress made, however little, in whatever sphere, and the positive points, however few. Remember, few of us go out of our way to collect Ds and Es. On the other hand, do not go overboard about the high-flier. Extremes of praise are as undesirable as extremes of criticism. Care must be taken with references to the balance between home and school contributions to the child's progress as well. The only safe reference to home conditions is one in praise of parental cooperation with the school in any way, or, for instance, of the fact that they provide the young child with books and read to him a lot, or that they have successfully encouraged an older pupil to join a school club. Suggestions of parental contribution along these or any other lines are probably best handled by tactful suggestion in a face-to-face situation, or a letter written with a tact born of experience. The class teacher/group tutor will need to draw together the general implications of the various sections of the report, and try to paint a rounded picture by taking account of the 'incidental' information available to him in the carefully kept records we referred to in Chapter Three. He has a duty to show, for example, why the high-flier is not impressing people favourably with his appearance, attitudes, or general behaviour, or that one collector of Ds and Es is well liked and respected by fellow pupils and staff alike. The last might be because he is always where he should be, on time, neat and tidy, polite, helpful, willing to do his bit, able to take responsibility in social situations, trustworthy.

Whether he reports in a pastoral role or a curriculum role, the importance of what a teacher chooses to put in a report is matched by the importance of how he writes it. We refer to his handwriting, his spelling, his choice of words and ways of arranging them. This is true, of course, whenever he writes to parents, and we shall show later that he must take as much care with his spoken language in meetings with them. It is obviously essential that the teacher's handwriting be legible. It is also very important that it should be reasonably 'tidy', for the same reason that his spelling must be correct, i.e., matching that of the Oxford dictionary. It is a matter of his credibility in the eyes of the parents. If he cannot see this, he has misunderstood a crucial aspect of the appropriateness versus correctness argument that he studied in his course on language in curriculum in initial training. It may not (or may) matter to his colleagues whether he spells correctly or phonetically, as long as they understand him, but it will matter to the parents of his pupils. They have certain expectations of teachers. These may be irrational (or not) but there they are. And, if the teacher cannot meet them, the parents will think the less of him and his opinions. When it comes to the vocabulary and syntax of his written communication the teacher must remember that some parents have reading difficulties by any standards, while even very literate parents are going to have some if he uses 'in' language. Educators have as great a facility as any other professional group for inventing new words, giving quite common words new and esoteric meanings, using an uncommon long word when a common short one would do the job, arranging some very ordinary words in such a convoluted way that the sentence is scarcely comprehensible, conveying the meaning they intended along with a couple of implications they did not. All these pitfalls await the teacher. One way to avoid them is to try out one's written efforts on a colleague or one's spouse, especially those that are intended to convey criticism without giving offence. There is a need to be careful about confidentiality, of course. It is all right for them to hear what you have written, but not necessarily to know who it is about. It may not be fair to the pupil for even the colleague to hear views or information about him, unless the nature of any contacts between them in school is such that the pupil's best interests are served by his knowing. For this reason, and because not everybody who enters a school is a teacher, there is a real need for the teacher to keep reports secure and out of sight at all times.

Neither of the reports in our example has space on it for written comment by the parent. Practice in this aspect of parent-teacher contact varies, as in all others. Another secondary school, which uses a booklet similar to the one we have described, includes an extra page. The parent is asked to signify receipt of the document at the bottom of this and invited to record any comment he wishes to make on the rest of it. This gives him as much space as the pupil's tutor and head of house have between them. The debate about such practice can be very interesting. Some say that a parent disinclined to visit a school might be more ready to engage in communication with its teachers 'at a safe distance', so to speak, others that it encourages parents to evade their responsibility to establish a close contact with their children's teachers. We wonder if it is not the case that those who really wanted to come would do so however they were invited, and that the majority of those disinclined to come would be even more loath to write. Teachers do, after all, bewail persistently that the parents most difficult to get to the school are the ones they most wish to talk with, those whose children have the greatest problems, academically and/or socially. It is interesting to notice about this second booklet that it does not give any explanation of grading, such as is carried by our first example, and to envisage that final page being used to request clarification. It is more likely, however, that the page would not be used and time would be taken up by explanation at the ensuing parent-teacher meetings. At the secondary school in our example the report is on classwork during the greater part of a school year and parents are invited to confer with the pupil's group tutor about it, with the housemaster in attendance. A separate examination report sheet is issued later, bearing only examination attainment grades and a reminder of how they are to be interpreted. Immediately after this, parents are invited to confer with as many of the subject teachers as they wish, and heads of department are obviously present. The report from the primary school is also about work in general, and parents can confer about it with the class teacher, with the headteacher also in attendance. These arrangements reflect the organization of the schools, of course. One could imagine a primary school with an unusual amount of specialization needing to adopt procedures closer to those of our secondary school example and a middle school needing to use quite different procedures for their pupils' first one or two years to those for succeeding years, to ensure that, as far as possible, anybody with a direct responsibility for a pupil could have some direct contact with his parents.

We have indicated already three aspects of these meetings that teachers have to take care over. We have referred explicitly to the teacher's records, and the language of the situation, and by implication to its duration. By reason of the number of pupils concerned, a teacher cannot spend very long with any one set of parents unless he is to devote a quite considerable amount of time to the task overall. The general custom is for such meetings to take place in school, at the end of the school day. There are variations. One of the most interesting in our experience was that in a primary school where the teachers devoted two successive Saturday mornings to the business. In our example schools the class teachers and their headteacher, the group tutors and their housemasters, allot two successive evenings to it. They begin immediately after afternoon school and go on for some four hours. The secondary subject teachers and heads of department devote one very long evening to the work. But, of course, this covers only one year-group. It can be seen that, depending upon his dual role, his level of responsibility, and how far across the age-range he teaches, the secondary teacher is fairly certainly involved on several such occasions. Given the need to strike a balance between this and other forms of extracurricular activity, and between a teacher's responsibility to his pupils and his right to some time to call his own, as well as the importance of conferring about a report as soon as possible after it is written, one can understand the emergence of the most common form of organization for such sessions. This is used in both of our example schools for the meetings following the delivery of general reports. A letter giving the dates and times of the meetings is sent to the parent. The time available for the meetings is shown in the divisions of ten minutes, and the parents are asked to tick the time(s) at which they could attend. One of those times is subsequently allotted to them. It follows, then, that the form of report which gives as much of the necessary factual information as possible, as clearly as possible, not only allows the teacher to put the comment space to good use, but also increases the possible value of the ensuing interview. It also follows, nevertheless, that the teacher will have to do his best not to let the interview overrun the allotted time, or a reasonable period when no specific one has been set. Care with some of the factors that would increase the value of the interview should also help to control its length. For the first of these we hark back to the writing of the report, and the care with which it was written. The teacher may have two Miss J.P.W.T. Robinson's in his class, but that is no excuse for writing comment about Jane Robinson on Jean Robinson's report, and vice versa. About the language of the report we have been fairly explicit. We only reiterate here that he should have been so clear about what he wanted to say and have said it so clearly that it needs no interpretation at the interview. It should have been written with reference to his clear, carefully compiled notes about the pupil, and the records should be with him at the meeting, opened at the right place as soon as the parents introduce themselves. They should now include a carbon or other copy of his contribution to the original report, the whole thing if he is interviewing in the role of class teacher/group tutor. It adds nothing to the parents' confidence in him if he has to ask them to remind him of what was written at any point in the report, worst of all, his own page. If, in addition, they have not brought the original, the whole affair becomes rather messy. If there is an appointment system in operation and Mr. and Mrs. Smith should follow Mr. and Mrs. Brown, it is not certain that they will. Nervousness on a first occasion should not be allowed to prohibit a courteous greeting to, and identification of, each set of parents in turn. At the very least this will prevent the first two minutes from being spent on a crossed-line communication about two different pupils, and at best establish a pleasant atmosphere for the discussion. If the report was well written and the interview begins cordially and purposefully, the parents will be able to concentrate on evaluating the justification for the teacher's written remarks. This he will be able to give confidently, by reference to his records if necessary. He can give them a lead by remarking, for example, that they 'must have been very pleased with Jill's report', or 'with the effort grades on John's report', or by asking whether they had been surprised 'that so many teachers had commented on Jim's poor general behaviour', or 'by the way Ann's effort grades lagged behind her attainment grades'. He is trying to ensure that, by the end of the short meeting, the parents feel that they have a clear picture of their child's 'other life', and at the same time that any help that they can give him in understanding any aspects of it that worry or puzzle him is forthcoming. It is essential that the parents are convinced both that the judgements on the report were made in good faith, in the light of the best available evidence, and that the teacher is genuinely prepared to reconsider them in the light of relevant information about, or interpretation of, their child's behaviour that they can put forward. We remember that one colleague was given considerable food for thought by the parents of a boy about whom he had written that it was a pity that he did not read more. They had to tell him that the boy presented only one behaviour problem to them; he persisted in reading in bed long after he should have been asleep. The teacher must not only value what he is told, but be seen to do so. He has been seen to refer to his notes of what he thought worth remembering about the pupil, he should be seen to be amending them in the light of information he says 'is interesting' or 'explains a lot'. All else apart, he will otherwise have forgotten most of it next day. It should be obvious by now why the teacher should use plain English plainly on these occasions. That excludes slang, jargon, esoteric vocabulary, and tortured syntax. Parents, like pupils, should be talked not at, nor to, but with. There is a nice balance between this and a teacher's sense of his own importance, or that of his special knowledge, in relation to that of the parents. We know that while British schooling prepares people for a great many skilled occupations, parenthood is not one of them, and that student teachers spend time studying childhood 'scientifically'. But we are sensitive to how little time even the longest teacher training allows for that, and we think that the new teacher should be also. He is entitled to believe that his knowledge of children, and of their learning especially, is probably better structured than that of most parents. It should be true that, in the end, he can make better judgements about that learning in the school situation than their parents can. He would be foolish, however, not to believe that, in most cases, the best all-round appreciation of the child comes ultimately to the parents. In the parent-teacher interview situation, he should be putting his judgements of his pupils to the test, not just handing them down. When the parents sense that the teacher has confidence without arrogance, and a balanced view of their respective contributions to the pupil's development, they are more likely to listen to, and try to act upon, suggestions about ways in which they might contribute at home to their child's progress in school.

The third requirement we suggested might be made of the format of a school's written report and of its information exchange procedures was that it should enable a teacher to obtain a first-hand appreciation of the experience of school from his pupils. We are not aware of any example of a successful attempt to include in such procedures an opportunity for pupils to comment upon their curriculum experiences in writing. To have the pupil present at the postreport conference is becoming more common. Our example primary school positively encourages this in the fourth year, the secondary school in the third year and after. This is because of the importance of the secondary pupil's selection within the optional elements of his post-third-year programme and of his studying them at the most appropriate level of difficulty, i.e., 'O' level, C.S.E., nonexamination. We have yet to be convinced that either in such situations, or indeed in schools' councils, the clients' evaluation of the provision for their educational experience is anywhere being heard, much less acted upon. We know that many of the providers have yet to be convinced that it should be.

In this chapter we have devoted most of our attention to report-writing and parents' evenings, forms of contact with parents that we expect most teachers to experience very early in their careers. Equally probable, especially in the primary and middle school stages, are open evenings. There the pupils' written work and their art and craft work go on display. So may they, in various exhibitions of their prowess in such fields as drama, music, and P.E. Increasingly probable, and again most common as yet in pre-secondary schools, are chances to have parents to work with one in the classroom. It is becoming quite common to have parents regularly reading with young children for instance, while having them to share a special knowledge or enthusiasm with the children as we instanced in Chapter Three is commonplace in a growing number of schools. Many schools are now quite accustomed to having parents assist with school journeys, upon which we commented in Chapter Three, and parent-teacher associations also abound. They not only support their schools by fund-raising efforts, but also provide opportunities for teachers and parents to meet socially, or in the shared learning experience afforded by lecture or discussion. The best of such associations can bring about a really valuable exchange of views and ideas and exert subtle influences for improvement upon a school's way of life. There remains, of course, the hard core of parents who never set foot inside the school. Community schools have opportunities to gently erode their resistance. Other schools may work on the premise that, while it is comparatively easy to ignore the circular-letter type of approach represented by such documents as report forms/books, and the sterotyped invitations that accompany them, it is less easy to ignore the direct appeal/ attack of a personally addressed person-specific letter. This approach is far from infallible; we suggested why when considering the parent-comment page on report forms above. For those reasons the new teacher is well advised to seek counsel of a colleague preferably both experienced and knowing the family, permission from the appropriate senior colleague to write the letter, and a second opinion on its construction when written. Express permission to try the tactic of last resort is also essential. We would be surprised if a very new teacher got it, and doubtful about the wisdom of his using it if he did. We refer to the home visit. What is, in the last analysis, an intrusion into a family's very private physical and personal domain requires very careful handling. The advantage of a direct contact with the home of a child having severe difficulties at school over that through a third party such as an E.W.O. is fairly certain. However, setting it up by the home visit calls for different abilities than those customarily acquired in teacher training. It is significant that education authorities favouring it tended to appoint somebody to a school on a part-time teacher, part-time visitor basis and to give them special training in the latter role. Of course, what the teacher does in this respect, as with any other aspect of teacher-parent contact, will depend a great deal upon what he finds that his school does in the matter and how long and how well they have been doing it. We have tried to indicate some features of it in such a way as to make it possible for a teacher to begin to take up our final, two-pronged suggestion about it. That is that he should realize the importance of establishing contacts that give rise to the three benefits we described, and that he should work through all the channels of communication in the school (see Chapter Three, Figure 3.3) to bring about any improvement that he sees necessary in the relevant procedures at his school.

CHAPTER SIX

SOME LEGAL ASPECTS OF YOUR WORK AS A TEACHER

In initial training courses surprisingly little attention is usually given to this aspect of the teachers' work. Yet in their professional lives teachers are very much affected by the law and a plea of ignorance is not usually accepted as a valid reason for infringements of that law. Clearly, the law as it applies to teachers is a complex area of study and it is certainly not the intention of this chapter to try and equip the teacher with such expertise that he can if necessary stand up and conduct his own defence in a court of law. However, just as it is valuable for a teacher to have sufficient knowledge to be able to carry out minor first aid in school without the necessity of obtaining a medical degree, so it is equally valuable for him to have some appreciation of those aspects of the law which affect him in his work without first pursuing a course for a recognized legal qualification. At the same time it cannot be stressed too strongly that should a teacher find himself in a position where it would appear likely that he is to be involved in legal action in connection with his work, then he should consult his professional association without delay.

In Chapter One we examined the procedures which might be followed in order to obtain a first teaching post and in Chapter Seven we turn to the question of moving to a different school after having gained some experience. Mention has been made earlier of contracts and the forms which such agreements between the teacher and his employers might take. Here we are concerned with the legal position regarding such agreements. Following a successful application for a teaching post it is the usual practice that the teacher receives two copies of an agreement which he is required to sign, one copy to be returned to the authority concerned. In the case of an aided school the agreement will be sent by the governors or managers. Needless to say, such an agreement should be very carefully read and the contents understood before being signed. The important point to note here is that in signing and returning the agreement the teacher is accepting the post under the terms offered and is thus legally entering into a contract with the employing authority to carry out the terms of the agreement between them. He is thus placed under certain obligations both in terms of the work he will be expected to do and of the period of notice he is required to give if and when he subsequently wishes to leave that particular post. In addition a teacher's contract includes a requirement that he will comply with the rules which his particular education authority enforces. Thus, in accepting an appointment the teacher gives an undertaking to comply with the authority's code and can be regarded as having broken the terms of his agreement if he fails to do this. Teachers newly appointed to an authority should therefore ensure that they are familiar with the particular rules set down by that authority.

We have previously given some discussion to the first year of teaching in a maintained school after completing training – the period being commonly referred to as 'the probationary year'. Within the context of this particular chapter some indication is necessary of the teacher's position should he be informed that this year has not been completed satisfactorily. Let it be said first of all that only a very small number of teachers fail to complete their probationary year to the satisfaction of their employers and the vast majority therefore receive formal confirmation of successful completion from their local authority. If, however, the LEA is not satisfied, on the evidence supplied by the headteacher and/or their own inspectors, that the teacher concerned has shown an adequate standard of proficiency, then the period of probation may be extended. The final decision to extend the probationary year rests with the Department of Education and Science but this is normally granted automatically when such recommendation is made by the LEA. When the period of probation is to be extended the Department of Education and Science will notify the teacher concerned, although it is generally accepted that the LEA should also first inform the teacher that such a recommendation is to be made. In the case of a first extension of probation the teacher is not able to make an appeal on the decision, nor is he necessarily given an explanation in writing as to why the period has been extended.

The situation becomes more serious if a further extension of probation is recommended, and if this occurs the reasons for the extension should be given to the teacher concerned. In such circumstances he also has the right to make representations to the Department of Education and Science before any final decision as to further extension is made. Before making any representation the teacher should first consult his professional association and ask for advice.

If following extensions in the probationary period the Department of Education and Science comes to a final decision that the teacher is unsuitable for employment in a maintained school, then he cannot continue to teach in such a school. He may, however, seek employment in an independent school – but most having reached this position would be well advised to devote their talents to a field removed from teaching.

Issues concerning the probationary year aside, we must appreciate that, having accepted and taken up a post in a school, the teacher clearly has obligations to that school and to the children who attend it. In carrying out his duties and fulfilling his obligations the teacher has himself a certain degree of legal backing. As far as the children are concerned some of the rights and duties of the actual parent are transferred to the teacher. This is what is meant when we refer to the teacher as being *in loco parentis* – a phrase which literally means 'in place of the parent'. The law recognizes that a parent should exercise some degree of care for his children and, as such, reasonable care is thus expected from the teacher. To go back almost a century but to a statement to which reference is still made today, one Mr. Justice Cave asked 'What is the duty of a schoolmaster? The duty of a schoolmaster is to take such care of his boys as a careful father would take of his boys.' The same theme has been echoed on many subsequent occasions – 'the duty of a schoolmaster in relation to his pupils is that of a careful father.'

Such statements, of course, raise questions. How 'careful' is a father expected to be and what rights are given to him in order that he may exercise such care? Furthermore, the teacher faced with a class of thirty or so pupils might well wonder how many fathers can claim responsibility for so many offspring! Basically, however, the law asks what is 'reasonable' in terms of responsibility for the child and the behaviour of the teacher towards him. In the following paragraphs we will examine a number of areas in which the teacher is regarded as having legal responsibilities towards his pupils and in several of these areas you will see that a key question to be asked is, 'What would be the behaviour expected of a reasonable parent?'

First, the question of safety in schools and the legal position if and when accidents occur. Of the number of children who each day attend schools throughout the country the proportion who suffer any degree of accident is relatively small. At the same time, however, we must accept that among any community or in any building potential hazards exist – one can slip and sprain an ankle while climbing the stairs at home. Schools are no exception and within the school environment there are a number of potential sources of danger for both pupils and teachers. All teachers should therefore be aware of such hazards as do exist. Prevention is, of course, better than cure. There is now safety legislation in schools as a result of the Health and Safety at Work Act of 1974. This act extended the application of safety legislation to include teachers and others in the education service. In terms of the act pupils and students come within the category of 'persons and other employees liable to be affected'. At present, however, the inspection of schools is something of a new area for the health and safety commission and it is not fully established what their powers of inspection will be and how they may be carried out. At the same time, some effects of the act are being felt in schools. Some local education authorities have now circulated written requirements on safety measures to the schools which are under their control. Teachers, therefore, would be well advised to check if such requirements are made by their particular LEA and, if so, the form that they take. Additionally, the Department of Education and Science has produced a series of six booklets which, although not intended for use in any legal sense, provide valuable advice and guidelines on safety. The six pamphlets (obtainable from H.M.S.O.) are:

Number 1   Safety in Outdoor Pursuits
Number 2   Safety in Science Laboratories
Number 3   Safety in Practical Departments
Number 4   Safety in Physical Education
Number 5   Safety in Further Education
Number 6   Safety in School: General Advice.

However stringent the precautions taken, there will always be the possibility that an accident will occur. In looking at the teacher's legal position in such a situation it is first necessary to examine the term 'negligence'. If, following an accident to his child, a parent wishes to bring an action against the managers or governors of the school, the LEA, or the teacher who appears to be concerned, then, to be successful in his action negligence must be proved. Like many terms 'negligence' cannot be briefly defined in such a way as to cover every possible contingency. What is important for the teacher, however, is to appreciate that for any claim for negligence to be successful three conditions must be satisfied. The law puts it this way. First, that the defendant owed a duty of care to the plaintiff. Second, that he failed, either by what he has or has not done, to carry out that duty. Finally, that the plaintiff has suffered actual damage as a result of that act of omission. (Here, of course, we should substitute 'managers' or 'governers', 'LEA' or 'teacher' for 'defendant' and 'pupil' for 'plaintiff'.) What follows from these conditions is that a claim for damages is unlikely to succeed in the case of what is strictly an accident since, by definition, an accident is an event which cannot be prevented or which could not reasonably have been foreseen so that steps should have been taken to guard against it.

The individual teacher must, however, appreciate that he has responsibility for his pupils in a variety of situations where safety factors may be involved and he is expected to exercise that responsibility. Some school activities offer greater likelihood for mishap to occur than others. This is certainly the case in lessons such as physical education and games, science and domestic science, and studies associated with technology. In these subject areas it is important that the teacher should pay special regard to safety factors and should also be aware of specific requirements which may have been set down by his own LEA. There may, for example, be a requirement that pupils should wear protective eye shields when using certain machinery in workshops or that particular experiments in science should only be carried out behind a safety screen. Even when such procedures are not required by the LEA the wise teacher should strive to have these recognized as normal practice in his particular school. Where the LEA has made such requirements, however, it is essential that teachers ensure that these are carried out. Furthermore, when any specialized equipment is being used, it is important that the pupils have been given clear instructions for the use of that equipment and that supervision is provided during its use.

Accidents can, of course, occur in places other than the classroom, workshop, laboratory, or gymnasium. Children of any age 'letting off steam in the playground' are just as susceptible to danger and even in a friendly game during 'break' accidents can and do occur. Here it is important that the teacher who has been designated to be 'on duty' is available during the period specified. It is appreciated that every part of the school playground cannot be kept under the eye of the supervising teachers but it is important that the duty teachers keep a reasonable check on activities. In addition, if the school permits children to be on the premises before classes start or at the end of the school day then, again, adequate supervision must be provided. Many schools now lay down clearly the time at which children may enter the premises and the hour by which they should normally have left the school.

In most schools a proportion of the children remain at school for lunch, either having a lunch provided in the school or bringing their own packed meal. It is important that supervision of such children is provided and it is the responsibility of the headteacher to ensure that such supervision is adequate. Teachers cannot be required to supervise lunch-time dining sessions but those who volunteer to do so are expected to perform their duties conscientiously. The teacher is thus required to take any reasonable precautions to avoid accident to his pupils during this period and, if an accident should occur, his responsibility is the same as would be the case in his classroom.

Since accidents in school may result in subsequent legal action being taken by the parents of the child concerned it is important that following any accident the headteacher or his deputy is told immediately. It is also essential that, in anything other than a minor injury, an accident report form is completed either by the teacher responsible for the child at the time of the accident or by the teacher giving any emergency medical treatment. Great care is needed in completing this form and the teacher responsible for doing so would be wise to first complete the report in draft form and consult his professional association. Clearly, information given in the report should be purely factual and no suggestions should be made that the teacher completing it accepts any responsibility for the accident. The nature of the form itself varies from LEA to LEA but, in addition to personal details of the child involved – such as name, date of birth, address, and so on – usually requires that detailed information is given of particulars of the accident, the nature of the injury, names of witnesses, and an account of any treatment which has been given. Additionally, the question is asked in one form or another 'was there any fault in the building which might in any way have caused the accident?' Such a question must, of course, be answered fully and truthfully.

It is not only within the boundaries of the school that teachers bear responsibility for the children. This responsibility goes with them if they arrange any form of outing for their pupils. The teacher in his early years in the profession would, however, be well advised not to arrange a school outing himself – particularly one which involves travel by coach or train – until he has had the opportunity to benefit from assisting a more experienced colleague in organizing such a venture. The potential educational value of such visits is well recognized and, indeed, the Education Act of 1944 states that pupils may be required to 'attend any class not conducted on the school premises for the purpose of receiving instruction or training included in the secular curriculum at the school'. It is important to stress, however, that LEAs usually have their own regulations covering school outings and these generally relate to matters concerned with the supervision and safety of the pupils taking part. In particular, the LEA usually lays down the ratio of pupils to teacher required for the duration of the outing and this should be strictly adhered to. Frequently one teacher is required for every twenty children involved and where both sexes are represented in the class a minimum of one male and one female teacher should accompany the group. Additionally, some LEAs require that parents give their permission for their child to be taken on a school visit but when this is not specified by the employing authority then the school is not legally required to consult the parents. At the same time, however, it is wise for teachers to inform parents before any outing takes place and this is particularly necessary if the children are likely to return to the school later than the normal time at which school ends. Some schools make it a practice for parents to be asked to sign a letter in which they give their agreement that their child may take part in the visit. Furthermore, a sentence is frequently inserted in such letters to the effect that in the event of an accident to the child the parent will not make any claim against the teachers concerned. Whatever the wording used it is important for the teacher to appreciate that the parent's signature in no way absolves the school if an accident should occur to the child and it is the responsibility of the teachers taking part in the outing to exercise the degree of care and supervision which the law expects of one *in loco parentis*. Such letters do, however, have the value of drawing the attention of parents to any possible risks involved and, in the event of any claim for alleged negligence, would be likely to weigh in the teacher's favour.

From time to time a pupil asks a teacher if he or she will look after a particular article of property. This often occurs when, for one reason or another, the child has brought money to school or asks a teacher to 'look after' a watch or piece of jewellery during a p.e. or games lesson. Teachers are often concerned as to how they stand legally in undertaking to care for such property. If the school authorities require that the teacher accepts such articles during, say, games periods, then the teacher is acting as an agent and is therefore not principally liable for the property. Other than this, it must first be said that a teacher is under no obligation as such to accept custody of property belonging to his pupils; it is accepted that the personal property which the child brings to school is the responsibility of the parents and of the pupil concerned. If, however, a teacher does agree to care for money or any other articles belonging to a pupil, then he is expected to take reasonable precautions to ensure that the property can be returned to the pupil. 'Reasonable care' is viewed as the degree of care which a prudent person would exercise with regard to his own property. If, as a result of gross negligence (which would have to be proved), he was unable to return the property to the child, then the teacher would become liable. To illustrate with an example, if a teacher agrees to look after a watch belonging to a pupil and leaves it on his desk in an unlocked classroom or on a bench in an unlocked changing room, then it would be reasonable to regard it as negligence on his part if the watch was stolen. On the other hand, if the watch was placed in a locked drawer which was subsequently broken into, the teacher would have grounds for claiming that he did, in fact, take reasonable precautions to safeguard the article left in his keeping. In addition, it is a defence if the teacher makes it clear when accepting the item that he accepts no responsibility for it.

It is not always as a result of the wishes of the pupil that a teacher takes charge of his property. 'All right laddie, I'll take care of that' is a sentence often used by teachers throughout the country and implies that the article concerned is being confiscated. There are various situations in which a teacher may feel it necessary to confiscate property. During the course of a lesson his attention may be attracted to a small group who appear to be showing more interest in the last edition of 'Kiddies Cuts' than to the lesson in hand and he decides to take the offending article from the children. A pupil may bring something to school which is clearly forbidden by the school rules and the teacher may feel that it is both right and indeed expected of him to confiscate such property. Another reason for confiscation is if and when a pupil brings dangerous or illegal items to school. Examples of these would include knives, alcohol, or drugs. Many teachers would view the possession of cigarettes, particularly by younger children, in the same way. Finally, a teacher may consider that a pupil is abusing his own property and remove it from him to protect the article concerned.

Having confiscated a pupil's property, what is required of the teacher by law both in terms of caring for the property and of returning it to its owner? Broadly speaking, it is necessary for the teacher to be guided by two constraints. First, there is his power to act *in loco parentis* and, second, the Theft Act of 1968. His position of being *in loco parentis* gives the teacher authority to remove an article from a child if in doing so he feels that he is behaving in a way which would be expected of a prudent parent. Thus, the teacher is perfectly entitled to remove property from a pupil for any of the reasons given earlier. However, he is also constrained by the Theft Act which says that anyone who 'dishonestly appropriates property belonging to another with the intention of permanently depriving the other of it' is guilty of theft. Here no exception is made in the case of confiscation by teachers. As a result of this act it is important that the teacher recognizes that (a) he is responsible for the property which has been confiscated and if he fails to take reasonable care of the article he may well have to pay for its replacement; (b) a pupil's property must never be destroyed; and (c) the property must at some time be returned to the pupil or to his parents. In situations where the article in question is considered dangerous or unsuitable for the child to have in his possession the appropriate action would be for a senior member of the school staff to write to the parents and ask if they would come along to the school and collect the article concerned. Thus, if you find one of your charges having a quick sip from his hip flask you are quite correct to confiscate the flask but have no right to increase your staff room popularity by pepping up the afternoon coffee with the confiscated goods!

In a very small number of cases the property confiscated may be an article which it is illegal for the pupil, or indeed anyone else, to possess. This would, of course, be the case if a pupil was found to be in possession of certain drugs or if it was believed that the article concerned was stolen property. In such circumstances the police may have to be called, but this should be the responsibility of the headteacher. When this action is taken it is important that the parents are also informed.

Mention has been made of a pupil being in possession of stolen property. It may also happen that a child complains that an article belonging to him is missing and the teacher has reason to suspect that it has been taken by another child in the school. What is the legal position if the teacher asks the accused child to 'turn out his pockets' or indeed wishes to search the pupil and the contents of his satchel or briefcase? Once again we find that the teacher's position of being *in loco parentis* comes into play, the only limitation of his rights being that he must act in a way which would be expected of a reasonable parent. The teacher should, however, be aware of any regulations which his particular LEA has made on this issue and in such cases ensure that he complies with them. Furthermore, it would seem commonsense to say the least that a male member of staff should not make a personal search of a female pupil but should ask for the assistance of a female colleague – preferably a senior member of staff. Remember, too, that even though a teacher is within his rights to search a pupil the parents of the child concerned may well write to the school and ask for some explanation of why this has been done. Searching children should not therefore be a practice undertaken lightly.

We now turn to a rather different issue – that of punishment. Again we find that on occasions where punishment of children would seem in order there is both legal backing and at the same time constraints on actions that the teacher might take. Once more, backing comes from the teacher's position of being *in loco parentis*, and this gives him both rights and obligations.

To quote the legal view, the position of the teacher is that 'it is his duty, if the child will not do as he advises it to do, to take whatever steps he considers necessary for its correction. But he must act honestly in this course, there must be a cause which a reasonable father believes justifies punishment.' Before administering punishment in any form, however, the teacher should consider the nature of the offence and its seriousness, the age of the child, and the likely effect of the punishment on that particular child. Different schools operate differing systems of punishments and, in addition, all LEAs have some regulations on this. Such regulations tend to deal with what are generally regarded as the more serious forms of punishment, such as corporal punishment, suspension, and expulsion. All teachers should be familiar with the regulations laid down by their particular LEA.

The two main areas of punishment in which teachers should be particularly aware of the legal position are those of detaining children and corporal punishment. In respect of the former, teachers do have a legal right to detain pupils. Whether or not this form of punishment is used and the way in which it is used will depend both on specific LEA regulations and the factors discussed above as applying to any punishment. Sometimes it is sufficient to detain children for only a few minutes after school in order that the teacher may 'get the message across'. This is very often effective with younger children and, providing the period does not exceed around ten minutes, there is little likelihood of redress. For longer periods of detention, however, LEA rules must be observed. These usually refer to two particular aspects of the punishment: (a) the maximum period for which a child may be detained; (b) period of notice which should be given to the pupil before the detention takes place. In the case of the latter a minimum period of twenty-four hours' notice is often the rule. This would seem sensible as it does give an opportunity for parents to be warned that their child will be arriving home late on a particular day (and why). In law, however, teachers do not need the consent of the parents to detain a child. Teachers are, however, advised to exercise a certain amount of what might be termed 'commonsense' in exercising their rights here and should bear in mind that, as with all punishments, any detention should be both moderate and reasonable. Thus, to detain a child with the result that he misses the last school bus which will enable him to return home without difficulty that evening would be regarded as unreasonable, and an alternative punishment – such as extra work to be done at home – should be given. This is a situation often faced by teachers in more rural areas.

Turning now to the issue of corporal punishment, it is important that we distinguish clearly at the outset the legal position of this form of sanction from opinions as to the rights and wrongs of corporal punishment itself. Here we are concerned purely with the legal aspect. As far as the law is concerned a teacher by being *in loco parentis* has the right to administer corporal punishment but the punishment itself must be reasonable and moderate. All instances of corporal punishment must be recorded in a 'punishment book' kept by the school. However, if the employing LEA have set down specific regulations regarding corporal punishment, then such regulations must be followed. Some LEAs – and the number is increasing – have banned the use of the cane either in their primary schools or in all schools under their jurisdiction. Teachers knowing that this is the case with their particular LEA who then disobey such regulations are in breach of contract and may themselves be subject to court action. Where the LEA allows corporal punishment there are generally clear regulations set down for its use. Not all education authorities, however, give copies of such regulations to teachers in their employ, although a copy should be available in every school. Many LEAs do not allow a teacher in his probationary year to administer corporal punishment. Others may restrict the use of such punishment to specific members of the school staff such as the headteacher and deputies.

It should go without saying that whatever the ruling for the use of the 'official cane' in a school the teacher should never administer any irregular corporal punishment. It may well be that a teacher's exasperation with the behaviour of a particular child leads him to feel that order may be restored by a 'quick clip around the ear'. However tempting the offending ear may be, the temptation should be firmly resisted as a charge of assault could follow. There are also medical reasons for avoiding this form of correction – what may appear to be a quick corrective action from the teacher's point of view may have far more serious consequences if the child is suffering from any medical defect which could be made worse by such a blow.

Mention should also be made of the wishes of parents in respect of corporal punishment and their particular child. It may well be the case that the parents object to such punishment and indicate their wishes to the school. The Society of Teachers Opposed to Physical Punishment (STOPP) has suggested a form which a letter from parents might take informing the headteacher and LEA that they forbid the employment of corporal punishment on their child.[1] The strength of such letters has not as yet been tested in a court of law but teachers should be aware if such wishes have been expressed by parents of children they teach and of possible implications if they should go against such wishes.

From time to time we have indicated situations in which a teacher would be well advised to consult one of the professional associations or unions. In order to be in a position to do so, he must, of course, be a member, and it is widely accepted that all teachers should give serious consideration to this and recognize the desirability of joining one of the several organizations which exist. (A list will be found in Appendix I.) A union should not, however, be joined simply as a means of providing advice and legal support if required. A member should also accept certain obligations which his membership entails. Meetings should be attended whenever possible – this is the teacher's opportunity to influence the formulation and practice of the policies of his union. It goes without saying that a member is required to support his union financially by means of an annual subscription. Tax relief is given by the Inland Revenue on membership fees paid to such associations.

[1] See Peacey, N., 'Corporal Punishment: a guide for concerned parents', *Where* 128, May 1977.

A further obligation which must be recognized concerns the fact that several unions are now not only prepared but have demonstrated that they will withdraw the services of their members from the schools in support of demands for changing educational policies or for increases in teacher's salaries. The only association to state categorically its opposition to strike action and the involvement of children in disputes is the Professional Association of Teachers. Should you therefore join a union which is known to be prepared to take such action then as a member you should also be prepared to join your colleagues in withdrawing your labour if required to do so.

It is in no way our intention to give advice as to which of the associations the new entrant might join. That is purely a matter for the individual concerned. In many cases a teacher will have joined a particular union as a student member during his course of training and wish to continue as a full member on taking up his first appointment. He may find that the membership of one particular union predominates in the staff room or, on the other hand, that there is representation of all the organizations. If the situation arises that the staff are almost one hundred percent members of one union and you wish to continue previous membership of one of the others, then the decision may not be an easy one to take. If you happen to be the only representative of one association in the school then you must be prepared to conduct a 'one man withdrawal of labour' if required to do so! You may also find yourself as the odd man out if your colleagues are required by their union to take a particular line of action. However, it is unlikely that you will spend the whole of your teaching career in your first school and the situation may not therefore be as crucial as might first be imagined.

Newly qualified teachers who are not committed to any particular union will generally be approached by those teachers who act as school correspondents of the unions represented on the teaching staff of the school. Such an approach will, of course, be made in the hope that you will join the union concerned, but it should also be recognized that school correspondents are provided with a wealth of information and should therefore be in a position to answer any questions you may wish to ask about the policies, organization, and practices of their particular association. The individual concerned should then make an informed decision as to which of the associations he wishes to join and, having become a member, give his union his full support.

CHAPTER SEVEN

FURTHERING YOUR CAREER

In an earlier chapter we referred to the headmaster who felt that it was only after five years of teaching that a judgement could be made as to whether or not a new entrant might become a 'good teacher'. Although the period of time specified might well be questioned we can nevertheless benefit by appreciating his recognition that the gaining of 'qualified teacher' status is very much a first stage in the teacher's career and that if he is to develop the skills and understanding of the true professional indicated in Chapter Two then much learning is still required. Certainly he must learn from his practical experiences in the classroom but that learning should be within the context of continued development and appreciation of the nature and process of education itself. In other words, as recognized by James (1971), the teacher's own education must continue long after his course of initial training is completed. During the first year of teaching it would be unwise to attempt further study which required a fair degree of commitment both in terms of time and energy but after completion of the probationary year serious consideration should be given to the value of – and, indeed, need for – in-service education. This can take a number of forms as will be discussed below.

Recent years have seen growing support for the view that teaching should be an 'all-graduate profession'. Teachers, however, are the first to recognize that the possession of a university degree is not in itself an automatic passport to becoming an effective teacher. Furthermore, what is meant by the term 'all-graduate profession'? Is the aim that all teachers should be graduates irrespective of degree subjects taken or that all teachers should hold a degree in which the study of education itself plays a significant part?

There is certainly much to support Kelly's[1] argument that the failures which some schools have experienced in attempting to implement and develop recent changes in educational thinking have not been caused by teacher's lack of understanding of their 'specialist subjects' but have frequently been the result of a failure to understand the process of education itself. Such understanding is unlikely, in all but a few cases, to be gained in initial training alone. We make no apology, therefore, for advocating that nongraduate teachers should give serious consideration to the value of part-time study to graduate or advanced diploma level in which in-depth study of education itself plays a prominent part. Furthermore, teachers who are graduates in other disciplines would do well to recognize the value of a study of education at a level higher than the postgraduate certificate in education.

There are many teachers who have continued their studies on a part-time basis. For example, over six thousand experienced teachers have now gained the B.Ed. degree from in-service courses. We must not, however, underestimate the personal sacrifices which must be made in order to do this. Such sacrifices can be both in terms of a more restricted family and social life and, depending upon the extent of support given by the LEA, of a financial nature. As a result, a married teacher considering a course of study which may take a number of years to complete would be well advised to discuss the likely implications of such work and gain the support of his or her spouse. From the school's point of view the headteacher (and in a secondary school the teacher's head of department) should also be approached and the aims of the work discussed. It should go without saying, however, that the teacher's commitment to his work in school must continue to take priority. Finally, it is often worth speaking to the LEA adviser as he is likely to be aware both of facilities offered locally and of any conditions which the LEA may impose if any financial assistance is provided.

The provision of facilities for part-time study leading to a degree or advanced diploma is by no means uniform throughout the country, either in terms of the course offered or the level of qualification awarded after successful completion of the course. Those living in an area which is served by a university, polytechnic, or institute of higher education may well find that evening courses for the B.Ed. degree are provided in addition to B.A.

Kelly, A.V. 'Towards a Fully Graduate Teaching Profession: the role of continuing and in-service education', *The New Era*, Vol 59., No. 6, 1978.

and B.Sc. studies. Frequently these are on a course unit or modular basis and, in the case of the B.Ed., credits towards the degree are usually given to those possessing a teacher-training qualification recognized by the Department of Education and Science. This usually means that the degree can be completed in three years of part-time study. Many institutions offer the possibility of gaining a degree at either pass or honours standard whereas others only offer courses leading to a pass degree. The implications of the latter should be appreciated at the outset since a good honours degree gains additional increments on the teacher's salary scale as well as generally being more favoured when one applies for promotion. Furthermore, teachers who later wish to continue their studies at, say, M.A. or M.Ed. level may find that an honours degree is a required condition for entry to the course.

Many teachers are attracted to the courses and unique methods of study provided by the Open University and this avenue may be particularly worth exploring by those without nearby facilities for advanced study or who do not wish to be committed to regular attendance for lectures on specific evenings each week. No formal academic qualifications are required for entry into the Open University but holders of a recognized teaching qualification are usually allowed to count this towards their degree. Each application for exemption on the basis of previous qualifications is treated on its own merits. The degree of B.A. is awarded in all faculties on the basis of gaining course credits – a student is required to obtain six credits for an ordinary degree and eight for a classified honours degree. Each credit (or half-credit) is gained by successfully completing specified work coupled with a written examination towards the end of the university teaching year.

The teaching year for the Open University lasts from February to October and much of the tuition is based on specially produced correspondence material coupled with set books, radio and television broadcasts. Each student is allocated to a tutor-counsellor who is responsible for overseeing the general progress of the student and to a course tutor whose responsibility is for the work of the student on a specific course. Written work is sent to the course tutor for comment and assessment and in addition many courses involve assignments which are computer marked. From time to time tutors hold meetings at a local centre and although attendance is not compulsory many students find this an ideal opportunity both for meeting others and for getting direct help with any difficulties which may have arisen in studying the course material. Further contact is also provided in some courses which require attendance for one week at a residential 'summer school' held at a number of host institutions throughout the country.

As its name implies the 'Open University' is 'open' to all, but there is clearly a limit to the number of students that can be accommodated in each academic year. Intending students are therefore advised to apply as early as possible – applications are accepted from January to June for the academic year which starts the following February – since admission is based on the principle of 'first come, first served'.

Teachers who do not wish to follow a full undergraduate programme with the Open University are often attracted to single courses which may be taken as an associate student. Several such courses are provided in all faculties, including the Faculty of Educational Studies. Last, but by no means least, are the opportunities provided for teachers to work for the diploma in reading development or to follow courses in mathematics or technology specially designed for those in the teaching profession.

Provision for the in-service education of teachers leading to a recognized diploma awared is also made by the College of Preceptors, a society of teachers founded in 1846 and given a royal charter in 1849. Today the college has developed and continues to develop a wide programme of advanced educational studies. Personal study courses by correspondence are provided or alternatively teachers may attend one of the many institutions of higher or further education which now offer part-time courses leading to the qualifications of the College of Preceptors. Qualifications awarded include those of associate (A.C.P.), licentiate (L.C.P.), and fellow (F.C.P.). The licentiate diploma is regarded as the equivalent of a university first degree and that of fellow as the standard expected for the award of an M.A. degree in education. In addition teachers may study for one of a number of specialist graduate-level diplomas awarded in areas such as primary, secondary, or further education, school management studies, special education, and curriculum studies.

A survey of the educational press will show that many universities, polytechnics, and institutes of higher education offer facilities for an advanced study in some aspect of education leading to a recognized diploma. Some courses permit the student to make a study in depth of one or more of what are often regarded as the contributory disciplines of education, whereas others cater for the teacher who may see his own career developing in a particular way. Thus, the teacher who wishes to have increasing responsibility for planning and implementing the curriculum in his school may decide to follow an advanced course in this area. Others may decide that their interests lie in working with children having special educational needs – handicapped children, disturbed children, and so on. Again, an advanced diploma in this field serves as a sound preparation when coupled with a reasonable length of teaching experience. Such courses may be offered on a full- and/or part-time basis. It is often the case that a part-time student attends lectures and seminars for two evenings per week over a period of two years while a full-time student completes the course in one year. In order to attend as a full-time student it is usually necessary to obtain secondment for the required period of time. Most LEAs will normally not consider seconding a teacher until he has a minimum of five years' experience and there is no guarantee that an application for secondment will be successful. Teachers considering making such an application should first discuss their plans with their headteacher – without his support you are unlikely to stand any chance of success. Most teachers are likely to be given secondment only once in their professional lives and it is therefore important that the course followed is one which gives maximum possible benefit both to the teacher himself and to the schools in which he will serve. Some teachers in fact feel that, where provisions allow, it is wise to gain a qualification at diploma level by part-time study and use a year's secondment to study for a higher level award, such as the M.A., or to pursue work leading to a research degree.

Our discussion so far has focussed on in-service work leading to an award-bearing qualification. This, however, is only one of the many forms which in-service provision takes and during his career the teacher is likely to find a variety of opportunities being presented which will help him to develop and increase his professional skills and understanding. Single lectures, day and weekend conferences, and courses of varying length (some during vacation periods) are offered to teachers. Sometimes these will take place at the teacher's centre; all teachers should be aware not only of the location of this building but of its times of opening and the facilities which it provides. Such details are often circulated to schools or may be obtained by contacting the warden of the centre. Not all courses, however, take place outside of the school – sometimes it is more appropriate for a course to be held in the school itself and this is usually arranged through the teachers' centre, LEA, or local inspectorate.

A further form of in-service provision – although one which overall effects relatively few teachers – is through what are usually referred to as 'conversion courses'. Such courses enable a teacher to qualify in a subject which differs from his initial specialism. At the time of writing, for example, secondary schools in some parts of the country are having difficulties in recruiting specialist teachers in mathematics, physical sciences, and design and technology/craft subjects, and courses have been established in several colleges to enable teachers to 'retrain' for such areas. Clearly, however, some aptitude for the subject in question is necessary if the teacher is going to do this successfully. There may well be vacant posts and promotion prospects in craft subjects, for example, but the man unable to fix a nail into a wall without dislodging most of the plaster might be accused of wishful thinking if he felt that his chances of gaining employment or promotion are increased if he should move to this area of the curriculum.

So far we have urged that teachers be prepared to continue their professional development long after initial qualifications have been obtained. No doubt this view will give rise to comments in some staff rooms of 'All very well, but after a full day in the classroom this is asking rather a lot.' We hope, however, that such observations will be few in number. Teaching can be – and often is – an exhausting and time-consuming occupation and at the end of the working day or as a weekend or holiday period approaches it is not always easy to find the additional energy or motivation to pursue further studies. Teachers, however, who argue that they have neither the time nor energy to keep up to date with developments in their own profession would no doubt be alarmed if their local general practitioner expressed the same sentiments for his particular work. We make no apology, therefore, for stressing the need for the teacher to be equally committed both in the interests of his pupils and his own advancement in his chosen career.

Let us turn, therefore, to the question of promotion and moving to a different school. From time to time we meet a teacher who, although nearing retirement, is working in the school to which he was appointed at the start of his career. Such teachers tend, however, to be the exception rather than the rule and it is generally appreciated that there are advantages both to teachers and pupils in gaining the experience which can come from serving in schools with differing organizations and in varied locations. Until fairly recently the new entrant to teaching who showed ability and ambition could set his sights on promotion either in his own school or by moving to another. The position today tends to be a little different with opportunities for relatively early promotion less evident. At the same time it is reasonable that the teacher with his career in mind should aim to widen his experience when an appropriate opportunity is seen to arise. There are no hard and fast rules as to how long one should ideally remain in one's first appointment –

certainly unless circumstances are exceptional it is unwise to attempt a change of schools during the probationary year. Most headteachers hope that a newly qualified member of staff will remain at the school for a minimum of two years and preferably three (there are of course exceptions – headteachers may occasionally be heard to breathe a sigh of relief when a teacher indicates an intention to apply for another post). The view is sometimes expressed that in his first year in the profession the teacher is taking far more from the school than he is able to give and is therefore expected to make his contribution in the years which follow.

A definite offer of promotion from, say, Scale I to Scale II is sometimes made to the teacher in his first school. In other cases those aiming to move up the ladder of responsibility are obliged to apply elsewhere. Before doing so, it is important to discuss the position with your present headteacher. Notwithstanding the fact that you will doubtless ask him to act as a referee, it is common courtesy to advise him of your intentions. Caution is needed at this stage if vague promises are made – many teachers showing some potential have been encouraged to refrain from applying elsewhere by hints of 'a possible allowance coming up in the near future'. This may well be so and said in all honesty. There is no guarantee, however, that the hoped-for promotion will materialize and unless a definite offer has been made in writing the teacher has no redress.

The procedures for making an application for second and subsequent appointments are similar to those outlined in Chapter One for those seeking their first teaching post. Some additional information, however, will be expected on the application form or in the curriculum vitae. In particular, this would include (a) the applicant's Department of Education and Science (DES) reference number; (b) teaching experience – name the schools and LEAs in which you have worked, presenting these in chronological order with your present post at the end. Give dates of taking up and resigning from the appointments and brief details of each school (e.g., approximate size and whether mixed or single sexed); (c) courses attended since gaining initial teaching qualifications. Again, list in chronological order and give the title of any qualification awarded.

Usually, as with first appointments, applicants are asked to supply the names of two persons to whom reference may be made. As we have indicated, it is generally expected that one will be the headteacher of the applicant's present school. Sometimes an advertisement states that one or more testimonials may be included with applications, although today greater importance is usually attached to references. Where testimonials are submitted it is important that they are photocopies and not the original documents and also that the writer of the testimonial is not also named as a referee. Once a new post has been found and the appointment confirmed in writing, it is important that the teacher submits his resignation from his present post without delay. The procedure is to write a letter of resignation to his present employers and to submit this through the headteacher of his current school. Although his contract will specify the minimum periods of notice required – usually two months when a resignation is to take effect on 31 December or 30 April and three months for one which will take effect on 31 August – headteachers will appreciate a longer period if this is possible in order that wheels may be set in motion for finding a replacement.

In the years which follow, the teacher who has chosen his career wisely should find that he becomes more and more established in his profession. Many will spend the greater part of their working lives in the classroom and without such teachers a breakdown in the educational service would be inevitable. It is often noted, however, with some regret that in order to improve his financial position the teacher finds it necessary to accept more and more administrative responsibilities which result in a corresponding reduction in the time spent in the classroom. This would seem certainly to be the case at present – what the future holds may be open to conjecture. Prospects of promotion within the primary school tend to focus on obtaining a headship or deputy headship, opportunities for secondary colleagues are usually greater in view of the larger number of senior posts in such schools (see Chapter Two). The teacher may, however, seek to continue his career in education away from the daily routine of the school. After gaining the necessary breadth and quality of teaching experience some aim for posts in the advisory service or accept an appointment as one of Her Majesties Inspectors (H.M.I.). Academic institutions offering courses in education can present opportunities for those with the relevant professional and academic expertise, although at present there are fewer openings in this field than was the position during the period of expansion of 'teacher education' in the late 1950s and 1960s. Other avenues in which the teacher may use his talents are wide-ranging – educational work in the armed services, adult education, education in the prison service, to name but a few. Whatever path he ultimately takes our hope would be that, in spite of the set-backs which, as in any occupation, occur from time to time, teachers maintain throughout their careers the enthusiasm and commitment with which so many embark on the 'practice of teaching'.

APPENDIX I

PROFESSIONAL ASSOCIATIONS

Assistant Masters and Mistresses Association
29 Gordon Square
LONDON
WC1H OPX

National Association of Schoolmasters/Union of Women Teachers
Swan Court
Waterhouse Street
HEMEL HEMPSTEAD
Hertfordshire
HP1 1DT

National Association of Teachers in Further and Higher Education
Hamilton House
Mabledon Place
LONDON
WC1H 9BD

National Union of Teachers
Hamilton House
Mabledon Place
LONDON
WC1H 9BD

Professional Association of Teachers
5 Wilson Street
DERBY
DE1 1PG

APPENDIX II

USEFUL ADDRESSES

Audio Visual Aids Centre
254/6 Belsize Road
LONDON
NW6 4BT

Department of Education and Science
Elizabeth House
York Road
LONDON
SE1 7PH

Local Authorities' Conditions of Service Advisory Board
41 Belgrave Square
LONDON
SW1X 8NZ

Pensions Branch of the DES
Mowden Hall
Staindrop Road
DARLINGTON
Co Durham

The College of Preceptors
Bloomsbury House
130 High Holborn
LONDON
WC1V 6PS

The Open University
Walton Hall
MILTON KEYNES
MK7 6AA
(Admission department is Box No. 48, Post Code MK7 6AB)

APPENDIX III

FURTHER READING

On preparing, carrying out and evaluating teaching programmes:

Rowntree, Derek, *Educational Technology in Curriculum Development*, (Second edition), Harper & Row, 1980.

On the availability of materials and services to assist the class teacher:

Treasure chest for teachers: services available to teachers and schools, The Teacher Publishing Co. Ltd.
Directory of Information Sources and Advisory Services, Councils and Education Press Ltd., for the Council for Educational Technology for the United Kingdom.

On the use of resources:

*Leggatt, Robert, *Showing Off: Display Techniques for Teachers*, National Council for Audio-Visual Aids in Education, 1974.
*Leggatt, Robert, *Lights Please: Using Projectors in the Classroom*, National Council for Audio-Visual Aids in Education, 1972.
Weston, John, *The Tape-recorder in the Classroom*, National Council for Audio-Visual Aids in Education, 1973.
*Hanson, John, *The Use of Resources*, (Teaching Today 3), Allen & Unwin, 1975.
*Trowbridge, N.F., *The New Media Challenge*, Macmillan, 1974.

On the subject teacher's tasks in the reading curriculum:

Alan, Robinson, H., *Teaching Reading and Study Techniques*, Allyn &
Bacon, 1975.
Herber, H.L., *Teaching Reading in the Contest Areas*, Prentice Hall, 1978.

On the idea that there is more to reading than meets the eye, and what to do
about it:

Walker, Christopher, *Reading Development and Extensions*, Ward Lock,
1974.
Potts, John, *Beyond Initial Reading*, Unwin, 1976.

On management and control:

Docking, J.W., *Control and Discipline in Schools*, Harper & Row, 1980.
Kounin, Jacobs, *Discipline and Group Management in Classrooms*, Holt
Rinehart, 1970.
Turner, Barry (Ed.), *Discipline in Schools*, Ward Lock, 1973.
Jones, Davies, Clive & Cave, R.G., *The Disruptive Pupil in the Secondary
School*, Ward Lock, 1976.

On co-operative teaching:

Warwick, David, *Team Teaching*, University of London Press, 1971.
Worrall, P. et al, *Teaching from Strength*, Hamish Hamilton, 1970.

On legal issues:

Barrell, G.R., *Teachers and the Law*, (fifth edition), Methuen, 1978.
Taylor, G. & Saunders, J.B., *The Law of Education*, Butterworth, 1976.

* Also contains useful lists of sources of information and/or materials.

INDEX

New titles in the Harper Education Series

Mathematics Teaching: Theory in Practice by T.H.F. Brissenden, University College of Swansea

Approaches to School Management edited by T. Bush, J. Goodey and C. Riches, Faculty of Educational Studies, The Open University

Linking Home and School: A New Review 3/ed edited by M. Craft, J. Raynor, The Open University, and Louis Cohen, Loughborough University of Technology

Control and Discipline in Schools: Perspectives and Approaches by J.W. Docking, Roehampton Institute of Higher Education

Children Learn to Measure: A Handbook for Teachers edited by J.A. Glenn, The Mathematics Education Trust

Curriculum Context edited by A.V. Kelly, Goldsmiths' College

The Primary Curriculum by A.V. Kelly and G. Blenkin, Goldsmiths' College

The Practice of Teaching by K. Martin and W. Bennett, Goldsmiths' College.

Helping the Troubled Child: Interprofessional Case Studies by Stephen Murgatroyd, The Open University

Educating the Gifted Child edited by Robert Povey, Christ Church College, Canterbury

Educational Technology in Curriculum Development 2/e by Derek Rowntree, The Open University

The Harper International Dictionary of Education by Derek Rowntree, The Open University

Education and Equality edited by David Rubinstein, Hull University

Clever Children in Comprehensive Schools by Auriol Stevens, Education Correspondent, The Observer

Values and Evaluation in Education edited by R. Straughan and J. Wrigley, University of Reading

Middle Schools: Origins, Ideology and Practice edited by L. Tickle and A. Hargreaves, Middle Schools Research Group